BICEPS & BUTTERFLIES

Biceps & Butterflies:

ADDICTION TRANSFORMED

Photo credit Yurino Koiso

Megan Johnson McCullough

Palmetto Publishing Group
Charleston, SC

Biceps & Butterflies

Cover Photo by Yurino Koiso

First Edition

Printed in the United States

ISBN-139781641116855
ISBN-10: 1641116854

Photo credit Yurino Koiso

Forward

Over the span of her four years of high school I met with Megan five or six times each year for half hour sessions to discuss her academic classes and personal issues. Megan was the star basketball player beginning in ninth grade. She excelled in all academic areas and was very focused on her goals. It was clear from our early interactions that she was an extraordinary person with a gentle soul. As her high school counselor, I was somewhat aware of the family dynamics and problems. Years later I attended her mother's funeral.

Megan did not speak much about her emotions in high school. A great deal has changed for her in that regard in recent years. Reading this book, I quickly discovered a woman with a remarkable voice. One with a capacity for making herself heard and understood through descriptive language and imagery. She courageously documents her life story recalling joyous, tragic and triumphant events. Megan bravely and fiercely opens her heart and invites the reader to experience her world. This is an enthralling, astonishing account of a life that is enormously shaped by addiction and survival.

Her intriguing capacity for truth-telling will leave the reader captivated. The book is a master class in highlighting the understanding of the child of an alcoholic. Megan is the observer and victim but ultimately the conqueror in this brilliant narrative journey she unapologetically takes us through.

David Anthony Lee

Butterfly Faith

Fly away to escape.
Stay let nature run its course.
Breathe let the heart calm its flutter.

Aspire to fly higher.
Don't drift with the wind.
The sun will warm the soul.

Transform, you're not finished.
She is in flight above you.
Your strength is in her butterfly spirit.

-written by Megan

Photo credit Lernik Elle Sepanosian

ALREADY HERE

Lyrics by Sarah Smith

Even the morning light
Can shine as dark as night
When you think that you've lost all hope
Your own light will guide you home

Caught up in the race
Caught up in the stress
Caught up in the heart attack

Already here
Already here
What you make of it
How you look at it
Everything you want from it is
Already here
All you want is already here

When you finally crawl out of bed
Shake off the day ahead
Same feeling every day
But you can make the change

Caught up in the race
Caught up in the stress
Caught up in the heart attack

Already here
Already here

What you make of it
How you look at it
Everything you want from it is
Already here
All you want is already here

No limitations
Light from darkness
Growing brighter
It's all inside ya

Already here
Already here
What you make of it
How you look at it
Everything you want from it is
Already here
All you want is already here

photo credit Stephen Smith

Table of Contents

Introduction

Exercise. Addiction. This is my story of a life disrupted and improved by both. When obsession and perfection collide, life carries a weight too heavy to lift. Catching yourself in the downward spiral has its saving grace, but the virtue of that talent doesn't always shine through. When you are your own worst enemy and drive yourself into the ground, no shovel can dig deep enough to get you out. Yet the human mind and spirit are miraculously resilient. That's why I'm here today. If cats have nine lives, I must have ninety-nine. Every curve on my body has been sculpted, but my smile is my best feature that deserves to radiate. I've found God, I've found peace, and I've found the courage to share my story.

This book is for my loved ones in the sky. May they rest in peace and enjoy the afterlife together. My wings of transformation have been built on patience and struggle and my flight has only just begun.

CHAPTER 1

Hey, I'm Megan!

Photo credit Kathy Magerkurth

Put a ball or pencil in my hand, and the sport or schoolwork in front of me means it's time to work. As early as first grade, when I played basketball on an all-boys' team ("biddy ball"), my competitive, perfectionist mind-set was in full force. The drive to compete at *anything* in life as well as possible was not a learned trait. I was born with it. With any team I played on, I approached it with the intention to be voted most valuable player (MVP) at the end of the season. At every grade level, I needed (and still need) straight As. It sounds like an incredible trait to possess, which it can be—when there are no disappointments or set-backs involved.

My favorite memories of early childhood came from my homelife, but my very worst memories came from there too. The cul-de-sac I lived on was every kid's dream. I had eight children all within five or six years of my age, not including my own siblings, as twenty-four seven play-mates. We had sleepovers, built forts, put on performances, rode bikes, and walked to the store every moment we could. We had a community of our own, and those neighbors were my best friends.

I spent a lot of time at the neighbor's house directly across from mine. It was my home away from home, with cooked meals and even family vacations that I attended. I was like the third sibling of the son and daughter. I was the youngest child by five years to my brother and by seven to my sister, so although I worshipped my sister and slept on her trundle bed every night and thought my brother had the coolest friends, we weren't exactly playing Barbies together. But at the neighbor's house, we played and played, and played some more. Looking back, I know why they readily allowed me to stay until 9:00 p.m., fed me dinner, took me to school, and treated me like their own. More to come on that note.

As the daughter of two incredible special education teachers, I felt that school was a priority, and teachers were highly involved in my life both at school and home. My parents' closest friends were their cowork-ers. My mom was well known for being the best dressed and having the best classroom decor. She made sure her children were the best dressed too. My dad was always coach of the year for basketball and bridged the gap between special ed students and other students on campus by having his basketball team players as aides to his class. My dad would take field trips to our house with the kids when he forgot his lunch, so I grew up having a special place in my heart for anyone who had a dis-ability—so much so that in preschool, I sat down in the special educa-tion classroom, thinking that was where I belonged. I had to be escorted back to my own classroom a few times per week.

My parents were the ones who had the snack shelf stocked, were still married, let anyone come over to the house for dinner, and let anyone sleep on the couch. Every Friday, my mom would pick out my dad's outfit to coach his game that night. They were a special couple, which to me was normal. I sort of frowned upon those who had stepbrothers and stepsisters. What was that about? That illusion changed. Looking back, I had wished for a long time that my dad would leave my mom and take me with him. More to come on that note.

My sister was the eldest. She was an actress and singer. My brother was the middle child. He was a soccer player and had a great social circle of friends. I'm the youngest. I played sports. We three were blessed to have private lessons, be on travel teams, have the latest and greatest gear, and go on family vacations every summer. My years up to age twelve were to be envied. My parents taught in different districts but aligned their teaching schedules so that every year we had a trip—Florida, Puerta Vallarta, Georgia, Hawaii, all over. Not to mention Disneyland or Disney World a few times a year.

CHAPTER 2:
Grandmas and Grandpas

My practically perfect parents were the results of my extremely incredible grandparents. My mother's side lived five minutes away and my dad's about forty-five minutes away. Those four people were my saviors, spoilers, and caretakers. My mom's mom, who lived close, held the title of "best friend" for me growing up—Grandma Marge. She was a force to be reckoned with and the sweetest woman alive. Grandma Marge was an original telephone operator for AT&T. Impressive.

Wherever we needed to go, she was the taxi driver, and whatever we wanted to do, she joined in. God, I loved her. From her bright pink lipstick, matching tops and accessories, daily walks, weekly hair appointments, and devoted care for my grandpa after his stroke, she was the most put-together grandma ever. Before I was born, my grandpa Bernard suffered a stroke that resulted in his left side being permanently paralyzed. His fist was actually bundled in a knot he couldn't open up. He was a large man, and due to his condition, he literally couldn't even wipe himself after the bathroom. Grandma Marge did it. She buckled his seat belt and was the caretaker until he just became too heavy and too difficult to handle on her own. I was scared of him in a way that a child is scared of a monster. He was kindhearted, but he was mysterious to me. Why was he so immobile, and why was his hand like that? He sat in the recliner all day and watched TV, never saying much. He ate in the other room alone because he couldn't sit at the main table comfortably. He was so different from my grandma. He hardly left the house, and she was active and outgoing every day. Bernard and I bonded over watching TV together. He literally watched TV from the time he woke up to the time he went to bed, and that was how he passed the hours of every single day. Well, I wanted to watch TV too, and we had some mutual shows we liked (like *Dr. Quinn, Medicine Woman*), but beyond that we had to share. We had a show-for-show agreement of CNN (mainly Larry King) and cartoons that went back and forth whenever I was there. He got to pick a show, and then I got to pick a show, and we spent many afternoons sitting there next to each other in our recliners being entertained while Grandma Marge cooked us dinner or got to read her magazines.

I attribute my routine nature to Grandma Marge. Her nightly getting-ready-for-bed plan was rigid; from using Elizabeth Arden creams to flossing and brushing with four different toothpastes, she took care of her hygiene with such delicacy. It didn't matter if we got home at 11:00 p.m. from my sister's plays—she had to uphold the hour-long process in addition to getting Bernard ready for bed. Every piece of jewelry she wore had its place to be returned, and she only washed her clothes every other wear. My husband and my sister's husband share a mutual joke about the Johnson sisters brushing their teeth forever and with paste running down their arms because we are so thorough like our grandma was.

I loved the routine of where we ate our dinners every night. Coco's for broccoli cheddar soup, Carl's Jr. for a Santa Fe chicken sandwich, San Marcos Lake for halibut and a spinach salad, Taco Bell for a Mexican pizza, and the European Deli for a pastrami sandwich and potato salad. Each week was mapped out. When I started dating Carl (now my husband), we went to Chili's every Friday night or some other restaurant over and over for a few months. I guess that saying "That's how I was raised", really does come into play. Now I even latch onto every Saturday; when I get to eat my one cheat meal, we go to the same place. Grandma Marge had a daily walking routine, and if the weather was poor, she would walk the mall over and over to make do. She was a role model of good health for me, and when I did get to go walk with her, it was her pace only. I had to keep up, which is a clear indication of my fast-paced walking; I get frustrated when Carl is lagging. I don't even slow down for my pugs, who aren't meant to go on marathon walks.

My mother was her only child, so they had a very close relationship, which transcended into her doting on us grandkids. When my grandmother's health took a downward spiral, I somehow grew hateful toward her. It went from my being her best friend and spending every moment that I could with her, to me getting frustrated when I would go visit her, and I would only stay for a short time. More to come on that note.

My other set of grandparents on my dad's side were amazing in so many ways too. They were the perfect couple, straight out of a fairy tale. My grandpa loved my grandma so much that he buttered her toast, cut her grapefruit, and made her fresh coffee every morning. She had diabetes and was a bigger woman, who used a cane to walk. She was so sweet and patient, but her health was poor. She hardly left the house. She even—I kid you not—sewed all her own clothing. In a sense, they were the opposite roles of Grandma Marge and Bernard. He took care of her. My grandpa (Pop Pop, as we called him) was a man I loved with every ounce of my heart. He was my buddy, but in my younger years, because this set of grandparents lived in Riverside (about an hour away), I naturally drifted toward my mom's side because they were part of my daily life. It was merely a matter of not getting to see them as much, but when I did, I couldn't wait to play cards with my grandma, color, and then go run errands for her with Pop Pop.

Each of us grandkids got a special turn during the summer to go stay with them in Riverside for a week or so. I remember Sizzler dinners and Toys "R" Us trips quite vividly. They did drive down from Riverside to watch our games and performances when they could. They never stayed overnight. One of my favorite high school memories was when they would come see my game, and then my dad's boys' team would play right after. Those Friday night back-to-back games were very special. I would get to sit in the bleachers with them and watch, and their breath smelled like onions. There was always an In-N-Out pit stop before coming to the gym; they didn't have In-N-Out in Riverside at that time.

Funny how you can remember the smells of your loved ones like they are still right here with you.

CHAPTER 3:
An Open Heart and Home

Myself, mom, and dad

My parents adopted the generosity of their parents. Many different players on my dad's teams and many of our friends stayed at
our house when their homelife was troublesome or they needed help. It
seemed like we had the perfect home and were those people that you
could count on, turn to, and feel like life was okay around. Our home

was a *home*. It didn't matter what age, gender, or race you were, my parents would bring you in and get you back on your feet.

When I was in the third grade, my parents even officially fostered one of these players. I had a new African American brother whom I nicknamed "my big black teddy bear." He was a junior in high school, so his stay was truly only the last two years of high school before he turned eighteen and went to college. But guess who had to literally give up their room for him? Me. I guess it was assumed that because I always slept on my sister's trundle bed or wanted to spend the night at my Grandma Marge's house, that it wouldn't really make a difference if I had a room or not. My Cabbage Patch dolls and American Girl dolls could be stored in the hallway closet. I was told it was only temporary. My parents got me a Disney Aladdin tent that I slept in when I was home. I wasn't devasted because until middle school, I probably spent the night at my grandma's house at least three times a week. Who wouldn't want to when you were the center of attention? I loved waking up to breakfast with butter and cinnamon on my toast, going to school and then straight to Baskin-Robbins afterward, heading home to watch a little TV with Grandpa Bernard, going off to practice with Grandma Marge (who parked superclose to the fields using Bernard's handicapped parking sticker so she could watch every second), getting dinner from one of her five places, coming home to a bath, and then getting tucked in by her. I was the only child when I was with her, just like my mother had been.

Grandma Marge wasn't the only lady I worshipped growing up. I was also attached to my mom and sister. You see, up until middle school, my mom and I were extremely close—even more so when my sister got into high school and had a busier social life. We had the same school schedule (two months on, one month off), so we had every holiday off together and summer while my older siblings were on my dad's traditional school schedule. That meant we shopped, we shopped some more, and we just went places with Grandma Marge. I clung to my mother's leg and had a shy nature about myself. Then I would switch over to my sister when she got home. My teenage sister was in high school, and although she stayed up late and had probably one of the messiest rooms ever (and she married a man who was just like her), I would crawl in at night and sleep there. She of course had to wake up earlier than I did for school, so I would watch *The Mickey Mouse Club* and *Looney Toons* while she picked out her clothes and did her makeup. She was a drama girl, so she sang and performed in every musical, and I wanted to see her in action every show I could (and we did, because she was my mom's favorite child). Although no one ever acknowledges these nuances outright, my sister and mom bonded over the performing arts, my dad liked me at the time because I was becoming a good athlete, and my brother was sort of a handful and kept my parents on their toes. Eventually when my sister entered the teenage "hate your mother stage," I was now the head honcho with my mom. But staying the favorite or feeling like I was my mom's favorite didn't last for long. More to come on that note later.

CHAPTER 4:
Fixer-Upper

Perfect looking mom on her wedding day

My mother had a need to always fix or improve what was in front of her. For instance, our childhood home was fully remodeled… twice. First, she had an entire upstairs built as an addition that had a spa bath and luxurious master bedroom for her and my dad. It was every parent's dream to have an escape from the kids downstairs. Then she had the entire kitchen redone with all the latest flooring. She also had every room lined with different wallpaper (which was the up-and-coming trend at the time). We had the biggest house on the block, a cemented front driveway done just so we could play basketball and skateboard on it, and a special treehouse built in the backyard. We also always had pugs, hence why I have continued the pug tradition myself. I currently have two by the names of Steve Nash and Phil Jackson. She did have a perfectionist nature. That house was special in so many ways, but it became cold and scary.

My sister, brother, and I were also her projects. When any sort of issue came up, her motherly notion was to fix the problem. My sister started this phenomenon by getting braces and eventually headgear. Then my brother and I followed suit when we were old enough. Okay, you're "of braces age" now, so let's go to the orthodontist (even if your teeth are rather straight already). Then it was acne. Oh no, pimples! Let's go to the dermatologist. Then there was the whole mental health, putting us on meds to straighten us out. My sister lucked out on that part (maybe it was associated with being the favorite child). We always wore the latest brands, too, no matter the expense.

In addition to being fixed by whichever applicable doctor, we also were given lessons to perfect whatever activities we took part in. My sister had vocal and acting lessons. My brother and I played on both competitive traveling soccer and basketball teams. We were extremely fortunate to have the ability to do all this, and I really never was denied any opportunities. My parents both worked full time, and my dad coached, but they made sure that we kept busy. We were going to be given the chance to be the best at whatever we wanted to become. Let's not forget, my sister also had dance lessons at one point, we all had piano, I had horseback riding and gymnastics lessons, and we all took swimming lessons. My brother got whatever toy he wanted, including the most popular types of bikes (GT at the time) and even a unicycle. My childhood was beyond what many ever experienced, and for that I'm forever grateful and know that it all culminated to help make me into the person I am today.

CHAPTER 5
The Game Changer

When I entered middle school, my sister had gone off to college, and my brother was finishing up high school. My foster brother had also left for college (he was the same age as my sister). For me, middle school was marked by the quest for popularity, wearing the latest trends, getting really good at sports, and then saying goodbye to that portion of my life. I went to my mom's school district until high school and then switched to another district in order to attend my dad's school. It worked out for transportation, but even more so for experiencing diversity and for better sports programs. I went from a tight group of girlfriends and classmates that I had been with since first grade to a whole new playing field. From sixth through eighth grade, I had a close circle of girlfriends, and every weekend we stayed at someone else's house. I actually did things on school nights. Some of them are still my social media friends. We never ended on bad terms, just lost touch because we went to different high schools. I also had my set of friends at home with all my neighbors.

The interesting part of this time period was that myself and my neighbors were all trying to be "cool" (whatever that meant), and we each had our cliques at school. I can hardly believe that my neighbors and I were not friends at school. Pretty crazy dynamics. My next-door neighbor, with whom I carpooled to and from school, was a stranger to me at school. We laughed on the way to school, but when the car door closed, it was see you later. Our school friends took priority, but that definitely was not the case once we got in the car and went back home. We never discussed this or even mentioned it to each other ever, as if that was the just way things were supposed to be.

But then, everything in eighth grade changed for me. *Everything.*

CHAPTER 6:

The Onset

My Grandpa Bernard, my mom's dad, the one who sat in the recliner, passed away. He lived to be eighty-two, which by all means was beyond expected for someone like him who'd had a stroke. Soon after this, my dad's mother died. Years of being an untreated diabetic took their toll. The smell of her gangrene finally forced her to go to the doctor. That went really bad really quickly (which is why she never went). The young doctor came into the room and said, "We will start amputating and cutting her foot". She said, "Don't you dare!" She died peacefully eating See's candies and still being my grandpa's queen. This meant my mom lost her dad, and my dad lost his mom. But death has a funny way of making or breaking families, sometimes increasing the bond and sometimes ripping it completely into shreds. For my mom, her father's death as an only child was the beginning of the end for her.

For those of us still living at home—my dad and me—alcohol entered our lives and became the devil of destruction. This was the beginning of an obvious problem, but a secret overshadowed by the formal years that everyone admired. The perfect family with the perfect house was headed into a hell of a storm that wasn't going to pass anytime soon.

Memory 1

My first memory of my mother's addiction was at an outdoor theater performance in which my sister had the starring role. The show had ended; it was time to walk to the car to leave. My mom couldn't stand up. She couldn't walk to the car. To avoid a scene, my dad basically carried her, kept his head down, and kept walking. People stared. That was the start of my dad making excuses for my mom. I was very naive to the reality of what ever really went on. My best friend from middle school was with us, and she just sort of went along with my story that she was sick. I knew something wasn't right, but then again, I didn't. The puzzle pieces didn't add up, but when you don't know what alcohol, sex, or drugs are, then you can't point a finger at concepts that don't exist in your world. I hadn't been exposed to any of these things, so if I didn't know what alcohol really was, how could I blame it? Yeah, my dad and Grandpa Bernard—even Grandma Marge—had beer, but it sort of seemed like just a drink kids couldn't have.

When she lay in bed for days, when she missed my sports games, or when she would fall down the stairs, my dad would say she had a sinus infection. Yes, a sinus infection. At that age, I full heartedly believed this sinus infection complete cover-up. It wasn't like the house had empty bottles all over the place, and it wasn't like she displayed obnoxious behavior if she had too many drinks at a restaurant or on the holidays. She would just drink upstairs in her room and hardly come down. She was a social drinker, but truly was a dangerous closet drinker who had more when no one was looking and more when everyone else was done.

Upstairs my parents had that built-on master bedroom with a really neat deck that overlooked the city. That room become my mother's dungeon. After the first year of the drinking, I did start to see those bottles. They were under the bed. She had a penchant for cheap vodka and the tiny little wine bottles. Even still, I believed that damned sinus infection excuse. My dad was only protecting me, and therein lies my very innocent nature; he kept my eyes oblivious to so much of what was surrounding me. Innocence may have been a form of denial or God's way of shielding me; whichever the case, it was my form of survival.

Memory 2

My second major memory of my mother's addiction happened in the blue minivan. I had gone to a girlfriend's house—mind you, this was still middle school when I did things like that—and I was ready to come home. I was always the last kid picked up. I just assumed my mother was always busy, which was a form of denial. Eventually she would show up and come get me. But this time, I called and called and called. This was prior to the days of cell phones, so either she would pick up or not. I wanted to go home, and I needed someone to answer the phone. She finally answered, and then I waited a couple of more hours for her to come get me at a location ten minutes away.

She pulled up, I got in the car, and my friend's mom asked if I was okay. I didn't understand why she would ask that. And then I did. We started the drive home, and my mother was falling asleep at the wheel—well, passing out at the wheel is more like it. Her head kept tilting to the side, and the car would steer to the side, and then she would jerk it back. I yelled, "What is wrong with you?" It was the longest ten minutes. Then I took my hand and pushed her head as hard as I could to wake her up. I hit my own mother. We made it home. I never talked about that night and don't even know if she ever realized what I had done. Maybe I should have told my dad. The rage I felt for my own safety and my extreme anger made me feel that the action was justifiable.

That wasn't the only time I got physical with her. I can't place on a timeline when the second event happened. But it happened. I pushed her down the stairs. There were so many times I just couldn't understand why she couldn't get herself together. I didn't ask for much, just to take me to practice. I needed something for a school project. Why can't you get up and take me? Or when she did get up, I had to wait another thirty minutes for her to even make it downstairs. I eventually cut her out as an option for anything. We had far exceeded the three-strikes rule, and my attitude changed from concern to just ignoring the fact that she was even there.

Memory 3

Other people had to be noticing her behaviors, and if they hadn't yet, my sister's wedding was going to get their attention. Oh, it was the perfect wedding in Calabasas. Traditionally, the mother of the bride does walk down the aisle. There was a really nice prewedding reception with cocktails and fancy appetizers. My mom had spent the afternoon sort of out of sight and then would stagger through the crowd and say hi to those in attendance. She had this black dress with off-the-shoulder sleeves. As the day went on and her drink count rose, I can remember the one sleeve just totally hanging off in that tacky get-yourself-together kind of way.

Now people were whispering. I can remember her two best friends were really taken aback. I can remember my aunt sort of giving me a look across the room. To top it off, her performance down the aisle was marked by my foster brother practically holding her up to make the walk. The show must go on. I'm sure some people thought this was an isolated incident, like she got carried away celebrating her favorite child's next chapter in her life. My dad and I weren't in shock, but I was sixteen at the time, which meant my brother and sister were not home to really know this was happening. Not only were our closest family friends exposed to this performance, but my siblings got to finally see how bad it was getting. My poor sister was so embarrassed but also unaware that this was a pretty regular occurrence at this point. Sometimes people drink too much, but this wasn't a sometime, accidental, oops-it-won't-happen-again type of behavior.

CHAPTER 7:
No One Talked About It

No one talked about it. Remember those neighbors across the street who treated me like one of their own? They didn't talk about it. They just took care of me. Remember that best friend who saw my dad carry my mom the first time she couldn't stand up? We didn't talk about it; she just invited me on all her family vacations to get away. Remember all those teacher friends? They never talked about it; they just kept being her friends but saw her less and less. Remember all those sports teams I played on? I had a ride to and from practice and games every time. Coaches and teammates' parents never asked why my mom's car was parked in the driveway and why she couldn't get me. They just made sure I had a ride and even fast food on the way home.

Remember Grandma Marge, who was the busiest taxi driver in town? Well, she picked up every ounce of slack for my mom. The funny part is, she believed that sinus infection crap too. How could her only daughter have a problem? Never. You can convince yourself of anything. So the *not* talking about it persisted. Again, my siblings were now away and out of the house, so there was no need to talk about it to them. The secret that wasn't really a secret remained undiscussed.

CHAPTER 8
Wildcats

I absolutely loved high school, even after being so intimidated by going to a new school with no friends to speak of. Those four years were the best years but were the worst years in my home. The addiction ramped itself up during this time period. Her inability to stop drinking drove me to hate her.

But no one had to know what was going on at home. I left every friend I had and switched school districts. Starting from scratch, I was fortunate to associate with the cross-country team the summer before school began. I made really genuinely nice friends and also played in the summer basketball league. Now if you know me, you know that I am a hard worker. And that summer, my mom's addiction grew while my quest to be the best grew.

Sweet Grandma Marge began to lose her memory when I entered high school. There was a quick transition from being so independent, so "with it," and so actively a part of my daily life, to feeling like she was incapable of living on her own anymore. She was my taxi driver for a bit longer, but then one day, before cell phones existed, I waited and waited for her to pick me up from school. She never made it. She forgot how to get there, so she just went home. Dementia had set in.

Instead of being concerned or saddened for her lack of memory, I got extremely frustrated with her. I went from calling my grandma my best friend to distancing myself from her. Why? Well, she was completely oblivious to what a terrible mother I felt that I had. For her, dementia was a blessing in disguise. She would never have to know that her one and only daughter was crumbling and falling apart. She went to live at an assisted living facility, and I visited her out of guilt and always left quickly after arriving. I felt like my mom was getting away with murder. Grandma Marge would ask me the same questions over and over, and I would just lose my patience. She would death-grip my hand and call me by my mom's name. I really flipped the switch on my sentiments toward her. I won't make excuses for that terrible behavior and do regret the last years of being too self-absorbed to pick up the slack for my mom and spend time with her.

Pop Pop, my dad's dad, was now in his early eighties. He had been living on his own in the same house after my grandma passed away. He eventually came to live in the same assisted living facility as Grandma Marge. They had different levels of care, so he stayed in the independent type unit. It was nice having my mom's mom and dad's dad only five minutes away. For whatever reason (and I really don't know why), I suddenly become hooked on Pop Pop, and our bond began to grow.

CHAPTER 9:
Love and Basketball

Mom and I after a high school basketball game...those bangs

Alife of playing soccer on travel teams and playing with older girls because I was performing at a higher level than my age group, turned to a life of basketball. I really didn't start seriously committing to basketball until seventh grade. Many assume that I played the sport religiously my whole life, but it was soccer that took priority for most of the beginning years. There's a correlation and a *why* I turned to basketball. Well, first and foremost, soccer and basketball are the same season at the high school level. That means I had to pick one or the other. Naturally, soccer would be the choice, especially considering I had an offer to try out for the junior Olympic team. But, as one parent who was my closet ally started to crumble, I desired the attention of my other parent—my dad.

Oh, Coach Johnson. The winningest *boys'* coach in California history, the most popular coach in Southern California, and every basketball player's dream to play for. How could I get his attention? Between being a girl and rather shy, what could I do? Well, shoot (no pun intended), play basketball of course. Not just play basketball, but kick butt at basketball to make him proud. I went from hanging on my mother's leg to being 100 percent daddy's girl. That cemented front driveway at home with the basketball hoop had no idea what it was in for. Now mind you, even though I was primarily playing soccer, in seventh and eighth grade I was the MVP of my school's basketball team, which was the standard I always set for myself. I was an athlete and blessed to be a pretty good one, so I just switched my focus to the other sport. So when my dad took a liking to coming to my games, giving me tips, and telling me he was proud of me, that made the decision to play basketball instead of soccer quite easy.

You know that classic assignment in first grade when the teacher asks, "Tell us about your hero"? My dad was all of that and more to me. What we experienced and saw together was unimaginable, unrelatable, dark, and scary, and it culminated with a final image and event I'd never wish upon anyone.

At that time, my dad's boys' teams had a legacy of winning. The girls' team at my high school was also on a streak of winning championships. Here I was, a measly freshman, coming into a program that had never lost a league game in over four years. But the funny part was, tiny little me (and one of two girls who were not of color on the team) could actually compete with the best of them. It was like, "Wait a second, I'm actually kind of good at basketball? Wait a second, I'm going to make varsity as a freshman? Wait a second, is my dad watching this all happen?"

The best part of all that was how some might assume that my dad was the boys' coach and teacher at the school, so of course I was going to get special treatment and make varsity. My playing spoke for itself, and all those assumptions were shut down quickly.

Set your mind to something, become fixated on it, obsess over it, go big or go home—the story of my life. That freshman year became the start of my perfectionism and aspiration to always be the best. But here's the thing—those traits came from my *mom*. My high school years were some of the highest points in my life but some of the lowest points for my mother. And that is where our worlds collided. The woman whom I clung to for the first twelve years of my life suddenly despised me, was jealous, and couldn't even make my high school graduation when I was runner-up valedictorian. How times had changed. But you know who did notice me? My *dad*.

CHAPTER 10
Glory Days

High school reminds me of Bruce Springsteen's classic "Glory Days" song. Back in high school, I was excelling and on top of the world. But while doing so, I was taking on that perfectionist personality full force and finding myself isolated by this lifestyle. I would practice basketball before school and after school every single day. Waking up at 4:00 a.m. was what had to be done. Staying up all night to do all my homework for honors and advanced placement classes was what had to be done. Nothing less than an A and nothing less than making the all-league team would be okay. I still hold three basketball school records at my high school. I told you, when I do things, I really do things.

My mother was a world champion baton (that's right, baton) twirler. She knew how to light up a room and put on a show. She had the beauty to match it. Her long bleached-blond hair and slender body turned heads. My dad was a lucky guy, no doubt. She took care of herself so well, but then no longer could. You see, when you are perfectionist, there can be a breaking point of total exhaustion from attaining and performing. My mother was the type of person who, if we felt sad, took us to the psychiatrist. If we had a pimple, it was, "Get in the car; let's go to the dermatologist." We all three had braces. It was her way of expressing love but at the same time perfecting us.

My ambition to be the best led to a world of total focus with everything revolving around whatever I set my mind to. I didn't attend school dances or have a typical social life that I once did in middle school. My mom would ask why I didn't have friends over. I wouldn't dare tell her I didn't want them to see her (even though they knew and didn't talk about it). Then again, there was no time, as I was too determined to practice and study, practice and study. She took this as depression, which in a sense had some truth. When you isolate you can have moments of sadness wishing for normalcy. But then came the sick and twisted world of my experiences with psychiatrists.

Results are addictive.
—Anonymous

CHAPTER 11:
Keeping Busy

Photo credit Alex Castro

I admit to being sad and knowing that I didn't enjoy or know how to enjoy life like those around me. But the sadness may have been just a constant loop of being worried. When you worry, you are forward thinking, and when you worry, you typically think the worst of some coming outcome or what could happen if...

Worry has been my life's greatest enemy. The demons of worry taunted me every day, most notably with the element of time. For me, time controls life's choices, and every waking moment of time needs to be productive and fulfilled. Productivity produces performance, and therefore, not a second can be thrown away napping, socializing, or relaxing. I went to bed exhausted but woke up ready to start the time all over.

This worry often led to little sleep, which led to:

Mom's Saying 1: "Even if you aren't sleeping, when you lie in bed and close your eyes, your body is resting."

As an adult, when I have a restless night or again try to coax myself from being worried, Mom's Saying 1 comforts my anxious soul.

Socially, I thought "hanging out" was a waste of time. Who hangs out with their friends? This was quite the change from middle school, when I had every weekend planned with my girlfriends. I spent my lunches in my dad's classroom doing homework or in his teacher friends' classrooms doing homework. These were adults being social, and I was the kid in high school doing the exact opposite. If anything, I considered going to practice and being at practice with my teammates as hanging out. That was my version of productively having friends.

Because I went to a different high school from my neighbors, I soon drifted apart from them as well. If they wanted to hang out with me, they could rebound my shots when I was practicing basketball. I can see a few of them smiling while reading this, knowing how totally true this was. I bounced that basketball morning, noon, and night, especially during the summer. Summer was the time to get better. I slept until 9:00 a.m. (I can remember this self-made schedule perfectly), went out front to practice until noon, called Grandma to help me get lunch, ate, went to the backyard, and did plyometrics with my Jumpsoles (shoes that promised to make you jump higher) and then the speed ladder. I then returned to the front when I finished to dribble some more. Then around 5:00 or 6:00 p.m., it was time to go to my summer league game or practice. Then my dad would pick me up, and we would go eat at Applebee's or Roadhouse (the restaurant where you could throw the peanut shells on the floor). Then bed. Repeat. I didn't get a tan from going to the beach—rather, it came from being in my driveway doing nonstop practice. My big lips and nose were toasted and bright pink regularly.

Many people assumed that my dad made me practice like this. The reality was that I begged him to tell me what drills to do, and I now chuckle at the fact that he said rebounding my own ball would make me better. That was a hell of way to get out of going out front with me. My parents had it easy with me. I never had to be told to do my homework or go to bed or call someone to get a ride. I was a young adult always on task, always on time, and I never asked for anything other than money for school or sports-related functions. I made my own lunch, picked out my own needs at the grocery store, and I listened. I will say that I didn't exactly help around the house. I kept my room tidy and did my own laundry, but I never swept the kitchen floor or did dishes. At the same time, I was never asked to.

Practice makes perfect and I've always had to prove to myself that I'm not a caterpillar, that I'm a butterfly.

> *My demons, though quiet, are never quite silenced. Calm as they may be, they wait patiently for a reason to wake, take an overdue breath, and crawl back into my ear.*

—Anonymous

CHAPTER 12:

Innocence Is Bliss

Because I was a truly good kid, it made it easy for people to look out for me when the subject that was never talked about affected my life. I had tremendous coaches growing up, who eventually learned the lesson that it was better to just take me home, even though I lived almost thirty minutes away (remember I changed school districts), versus waiting for my mom to ever show up. They would pull up to my driveway, see her car, tell me to have a good night, and that was that. I was a coach's daughter, and my parents were teachers, so I was very coachable, respectful, and so innocent.

I even looked innocent. I had bangs cut straight across my forehead until senior year. Such an outdated look. I didn't start my period until I was eighteen. I never kissed a boy until I was eighteen. I never wore makeup until college. And the biggest innocence of them all was that I believed in those sinus infections. I had buried myself in meticulous routines to meet my goals, which kept what was going on upstairs at a distance. It wasn't just me who didn't like to be home. My dad didn't either. My brother and sister were away at college, so he and I began the bond of basketball and tag-teaming everywhere together. We were barely home. We would be at basketball until eight o'clock at night, go to eat, and bring my mom something home to eat, and then it was practically time to just go to bed. The avoidance and not talking about it continued.

Then we started having to take her to the emergency room at least once a week. The binges became more frequent and heavier. So now it was 9:00 p.m., we had just gotten home, and my dad would tell me to get in the car, and then we would go take her to the hospital. At the time, yes, I thought it was a sinus infection gone wrong. If only. Interesting how he had me go every time, but that was just it—we survived those experiences because we had each other.

This led to difficulty getting to school on time the next day. Well, there were a couple of reasons for that. As mentioned, my parents were very generous, serving as a mom, a dad, and a coach to a number of children. My dad and I picked up three people on the way to school every morning. That was a setup to be late. Plus, we would get a late start. I would get up to do my shooting drills, but all the drama was taking its toll on my dad, so he crawled out of bed to get the day going. Mind you, he was sleeping next to her (or for that matter, not sleeping) when all of this occurred. But again, when we arrived late to school daily, my dad was never reprimanded. I was never told that I would get detention. My first-period teacher and the administration knew what was going on but never talked about. I think of this silence as a blessing because no one ever made me feel uncomfortable, or treated me like a victim, or made me feel like I needed to be asking for exceptions. It goes back to being a good kid. What was my first-period teacher going to say to the "perfect" student for being late and taking the seat closest to the door to not disrupt the class? No need for words.

CHAPTER 13:
Jealousy

When my mom was on her way down, I was on my way up. It didn't take a psychiatrist to tell me that my mom was jealous of me. Her purpose was dwindling, and after she lost her teaching job, her life had become a series of AA meetings and pacing around the house, but mainly lying in bed. I was now captain of my winning high school basketball team, had a 4.2 GPA, and spent practically every waking hour with my dad. The attention was on me, but more importantly, my dad's attention was on me. She hated that. She needed to be the number one female in his life, even if the competition was her own daughter. We went to school together, had the bond of basketball together, and went out to eat every night together.

When your own mother resents you, addict or not, it is a terrible feeling. My dad would try to say things like, "Go take your mom her food; she will like that." My rebuttal would be "No, she hates me, Dad. I don't want to go up there." My mom and I were competing for the same man. This put my dad in the middle between still being a husband and being a dad and mom to me at the same time. I just came to terms with their relationship (he would listen to whatever she said) and really tried to ignore some of the downright awful remarks she would make. I would be getting ready for school and come upstairs for toothpaste or some toiletry, and she would say, "I'm sure you want to watch him shower" or "Why don't you get dressed in front of him too?" Sick and twisted. Whether she was sober or not, those remarks were hurtful.

Oh yeah, let's not forget when she called the cops on me.

I lost respect for my mom and didn't listen to her if she ever tried telling me what to do. "You need to do this or that" didn't work for me anymore. I was a good kid, but I was a teenager too. I also didn't think she had any credibility. Here she was, three DUIs deep, and she called the cops on me. Oh yes, she did. I needed a ride to practice. She couldn't take me due to intoxication. Dad was gone. It was too late to call Grandma Marge now. So I took the minivan and drove myself (I had no license). Now, this was not my first time taking myself when I had to. It was the first time she cared that I did it. She called the police. They came to my practice, interrupted practice, asked to speak with my coach, pulled me outside, asked me what I had done, told me I could be arrested, and then said I needed to get a ride home. I walked back into practice. Everyone sort of laughed because I was the most innocent person they knew. I couldn't believe she had done that—I still can't—and that was my first run-in with the law.

Such negative memories overpower the good ones. And so many of my "good" memories are before the eighth grade, when I was too young to remember them wholeheartedly now. It's like taking your kids on exotic trips when they are young. It's better to wait until they are older and will remember. Sure, I can laugh that my own mom called the cops on me. The lesson could have been taught a different way, but so be it. I knew she was fighting demons and was losing the fight.

CHAPTER 14

The Only Exception

B ecause we were never home, some might say that was my dad's way of protecting me and saving what marriage he had. Some might say that drove her to further depression and more drinking. She was alone a lot. There is no right or wrong way to deal with someone who has an addiction. Any outside input is just an opinion that is usually unrealistic. Until you are right smack in the middle of it, the decisions you make are partly out of love for that person and partly just survival tactics. There is no quick fix, no way to force or make that person change, yet the world around seems to think they have the answers. Now, when people tell me about the addicts in their lives, be it their children or family members, I never pass judgment on what road they take in dealing with it.

The word *can't* is not in my vocabulary. I don't even let me clients tell me they can't do something. There is always a modification or accommodation for any age, ability, and level of comfort. There is *one exception* to this rule I've created: we can't change addicts. It's the justifiable time to use the word "can't." Rehab is not a guaranteed fix. Being sober for an extended period of time isn't a guaranteed fix. Taking medications that can block the effects of alcohol are still experimental and are not a guaranteed fix. What is guaranteed is that there will be chaos, there will be no clear answer, and you will feel a spectrum of emotions on any given day toward the addict. Recovery is a choice for the addict; they must decide. No one can do it for them.

CHAPTER 15

Old Soul Personality

Photo credit Kathy Magerkurth

The result of this home environment was that I became an old soul and mature beyond my years. Most kids would run to their counselor or teacher or confide in a friend about what was going on at home. Me, I knew she didn't mean it. I knew her actions were alcohol laced. What happens when you are around addicts is that your sense of normalcy becomes very distorted. Your tolerance for crazy also is really high. As a result, today, not much excites me, not much shocks me, and

I'm numb to a lot of emotion. What I do lack is empathy. After this trauma, not much seems intolerable. I don't cry when people die or pets die, I don't have happy tears, and I don't really find the need to hug other people. I guess that's called affection. I'm hard up with a shield, guarded, and I live by the notion that what I don't know can't hurt me.

I got the nickname "Eeyore" for a reason. Yes, I did get happy tears when I got married. Yes, some movies are tearjerkers. Yes, I stub my toe and cry (that hurts!). I do stink at girl talk. I do stink at hearing about my husband's day. Emotion takes up space and time. Just keep going. Keep working. When in truth, all this means is just keep hiding from knowing anything.

CHAPTER 16:
The Dark

I can't exactly explain *why*, but I've *always* been scared of the dark. Bad things happen in the dark. Bad things have not happened to me in the dark, but my mind is set on this association. At age thirty-three, I still meddle with sleeping with the light on. Growing up, my dad told me I wouldn't grow if I slept with the light on, so I'd fight it. He would tuck me in, I'd last a few minutes, and then I'd have to turn the light back on. This is why I slept on my sister's trundle bed or even went upstairs to my parents to sleep on the floor with my blanket. I never suffered from nightmares or had some sort of traumatic event in the dark, but I had a fear of opening my eyes and seeing something terrible in front of me, like a ghost or kidnapper. Today those same fears remain and having a light on seems to be the only way to sleep soundly. If someone else is in the room, I'm okay with no light. But my husband is a night owl, so until he arrives, it's lights on for sure. Now I torment with the idea that if it is dark and I open my eyes, I might see my mom's ghost.

CHAPTER 17:
Time to Go

For four years in high school, all I wanted to do was earn a college scholarship to play basketball and compete at the next level. That was my total goal. That was why I woke up early every morning, practiced nonstop, and went above and beyond to excel at the sport. There were a couple of local San Diego colleges that recruited me and that I could have gone to, but they weren't the ideal scenario. One only gave academic scholarships, not athletic, and at the other I would not have gotten a lot of playing time. I would have to understand my role as more of a practice player who may or may not get into the actual games. For me, that was a hard pill to swallow, and I wanted to play.

I took a visit to Denver, Colorado, to a school called Metro State. It was Division II, which to me seemed okay, even if all of my friends were going to big-name Division I schools. I wanted to play, and if I was going to have all expenses paid, well, that was a major consideration. I practiced with the team and got a tour of the city, and it seemed like I could really excel there. My dad, being the basketball guru that he was, knew the men's coach, who was from California, and the athletic director happened to have gone to college in California. There were a few connections that persuaded me to choose Denver. I don't know that when you are seventeen or eighteen, you should be making any life-changing decisions, but I signed the contract and had one week after high school graduation to get there for summer league.

Between the homelife situation, my total love for basketball, and the lack of people I needed to say goodbye to (I didn't have any close friends), I was ready for the quick transition and new life. I imagined being a whole new me in Colorado, where no one would have to know about my mom.

If nothing ever changed, there would be no butterflies. This girl was ready for change.

CHAPTER 18:
Taking the Driver's Seat

I had waited until I was eighteen to start driving, which is why I always needed those rides places. My dad worked at my school, so there was no pressing need to drive, and taking driver's ed was pretty much off the table since I had practice and games every weekend. Waiting until I was eighteen wouldn't require the class, and I could just go take the behind-the-wheel and written exams. Well, now I had about a week after high school graduation to get my driver's license because I did want to drive in Colorado. It was time I grew up, too, and started driving.

I was a little troubled by how hard I had to press my parents to get me a car. My sister had gotten a car at sixteen; so did my foster brother, and my brother got my dad's old car. So why, after being runner-up valedictorian and getting all my expenses paid for college, was it an area of contention to get me a car? My mom's resentment toward me had a lot to do with it, which I understood. Her sentiments toward me could vary from buying my love to telling me I needed to start paying rent. Eventually they got me a used Ford Ranger, and now I just needed the ability to drive it. Getting a DMV appointment quickly was the next step. Nothing close was open, so my dad took me to San Clemente, which was about thirty minutes away. We practiced and I had been driving a bit out of necessity (which the cops knew now). I felt ready. The written test was passed, and now I just needed the behind-the-wheel component.

On attempt number one, I failed. Failed. Automatic fail, actually. The instructor asked me to pull over into a parallel parking space. That was fine. Now it was time to exit and pull back out into traffic. He asked, "Okay, now where would you look first?" I said I'd look up into the rearview mirror and see if any cars were coming from behind me. Nope. Wrong answer. He told me you have to turn around and look over your shoulder first. Well, I'll be damned. He said we would have to go back to the building right away and I could reschedule. Sure, why not? I only had a week.

Again, nothing close was available for me to retest. There was an appointment in Simi Valley, which was maybe thirty minutes from my sister's house. I called her. She said get on the train. Lucky me, she had my mom's minivan because her car was being worked on. I was a pro at driving that van, and since you drive your own car for the test, it seemed like the stars aligned to make it happen. We went to the DMV the next day. Lo and behold, we are all ready to go, and the instructor comes to get me and tells us the back-brake light is out on the vehicle. This meant the minivan could not be used for the test. Are you serious? He said, "Go get it fixed, and I'll get you back in here this afternoon." All right, let's go get if fixed. Two blondes with no mechanical knowledge to speak of were now on a mission to get the light replaced. Anything else? We got it fixed, I came back, I passed, and then I got on the train now with just a couple of days left at home.

I packed my life up. My dad and I loaded up the Ford Ranger, and we made the sixteen-hour drive to Denver. We were newbies to driving the mountains to get there, and when we hit Aspen, our amateur status got the best of us. Dad had done most of the driving, and now we were on a two-lane road creeping up the mountain passes when it started to heavily rain and lightly snow. Um, snow? Dad panicked. We had to pull over. Now it was my turn to drive. Sure, I had my license now, right? Death-gripping the wheel, window wipers full speed ahead, and sitting on the edge of the driver's seat, we made it. Tired and getting in late, we pulled into downtown Denver. We got a hotel and went to a cowboy bar to eat, and then the next day, my dad took a plane home.

CHAPTER 19:

Denver Days

Hello, Denver! That summer the coaches had arranged for me to stay with some teammates at their condo until school time came and my living arrangements were settled. We had summer league games a couple of times a week at night; then I really had nothing else to do. I got a gym membership and tanning membership and just did both pretty much all day every day. I kept wanting to improve and had nothing but the time to do it. What was great about that summer was that I proved myself to my team that I was going to be a valuable asset. I was easy to get along with and just wanted to win.

I will say that between high school and college, I knew many of my teammates respected me for my drive to be the best. I earned my playing time no doubt.

When the season rolled around, I was the starting point guard. I did play practically the entire games. I was the big fish in a small pond, loving every single minute of it. I would call my dad after every game and give him my stats. My Denver decision was panning out—until I tore my ACL and meniscus. Indestructible me—superfit, all-muscle me—went up for a layup on a fast break and got taken down. I screamed bloody murder. I had never, ever, experienced an injury like this.

CHAPTER 20:
Freshman Fifty

Weight gain definitely happened

For a gal who thought basketball was her world, this was a devasting, life-changing moment. The MRI confirmed the injury, and surgery was scheduled once the swelling subsided. My parents and sister flew out, and my mom stayed a couple of extra days since she wasn't working. She should not have come at all. Our family friend's son was attending college in Boulder, Colorado, which was about thirty minutes away. We had grown up side by side (hence why we both went to Colorado). I had to ask him to come stay with my mom and me once my dad and sister went home because she was too out of it to really help me. He came and even washed my hair in the sink for me, and he helped me get her back to the airport.

From being an exercise addict to now being immobile, I was troubled not only physically by this injury, but it presented a whole new realm of mental confusion. With basketball taken away, and for who knows how long, what was I going to do or become? I couldn't even rotate the pedal on a stationary bike. Talk about square one.

Food became very comforting. The trouble was, I wasn't very active for the time being. Unless you are aware at age eighteen that you should eat less to compensate for little movement (yeah, right), the pounds start packing on. Freshman fifteen? Try freshmen fifty. Seriously. When I flew home for Christmas, a few heads turned at my new round face and bigger self.

The other caveat to this injury was that I did not qualify for a medical red shirt, which would have allowed me to regain that freshman year of eligibility to play. I had played two games over the cutoff. Food, please.

When the new semester started for school that fall, I decided to figure this out. My clothes weren't fitting me, my grades stunk, and all I wanted to do was go home. I did in fact beg my parents to let me go home. I had had a few really high-scoring games against some California teams when we played them, and I was convinced I could transfer and get back home. No, my parents were the type who always said we had to finish what we started. Happy or not, I was going to stick it out. Happy or not, I could not come home until I graduated. If that was going to be the case, then I better figure out how to recover quicker and get back to playing. My coach had started recruiting, and I feared being replaced.

I arranged my classes so that I went very early (close to 7:00 a.m.) and then had night classes. This created a huge gap in my day. That gap was spent in the physical training room doing exercises and ice baths nonstop. My knee was held in a bent position post-surgery, so part of rehabilitation was getting that knee to straighten out. I would lay on the table, and the trainer would put all his weight and force pushing down on my knee, holding it for increments of time in the straight position. I would literally scream into a pillow. I was going to come back quicker, faster, and stronger; I would get the extra weight off and get my spot back.

And that is exactly what I did, until the politics of the sport practically ruined my final two years, and even my dad knew sometimes you can be a top player, but sometimes the sport isn't always just about the sport. I went from all minutes to no minutes in the games. I was ready, more than ever before, to get out of Denver.

The injury opened up my eyes to what life was without basketball. I had learned that my identity still existed even without the sport. I had become practically a live-in nanny for the athletic director at my school, and that job filled my time and let me earn some income during my final year. I had met with the AD, and we basically fast-tracked me out of there to graduate. My scholarship would have covered five years of school, but I was headed out in three. I went from being the girl who wanted to make it to the pros to the girl who wanted to hang up her shoes, go home, and start a career. Basketball had left a bad taste in my mouth from college.

I was so disgusted that when I came home and tried to just play for fun, it wasn't fun—so much so, that watching it on TV couldn't hold my attention. So much so, that even though I liked going to my dad's games, if it weren't for him having me film the games, I would have passed on going. When I did coach after college, the dramatics and politics were now more noticeable to me. Couldn't we just play? I tried for a long time to get a teaching job and coaching job, which would have been a great combination, following in my dad's footsteps. I kept getting false promises of offers for teaching as long as I was the coach, but that never panned out. I couldn't live off the pennies I was making coaching, so I hung up those laces and clipboard after about two years. Today, I might watch the Lakers if the game isn't on too late. I might go to one of my dad's games, but I'm not excited about either anymore. Just something to do.

Perhaps the butterfly is proof you can go through a great deal of darkness yet become something beautiful.

—Anonymous

CHAPTER 21:

The Boys before Carl

My very few relationships prior to my Carl (my husband) were
marked by me being absolutely head over heels for those guys.
Postinjury, I finally looked up more and took notice of males. I had become approachable—not just the basketball, school, best-dressed, don't-
talk-to-me-I-don't-have-time girl. My first long-term (if you call it long
term) and actual real boyfriend lasted about six months. He was fun
and athletic, and he was my first love. When we broke up, I didn't know
what to do with myself. Ironically, my mom said she would come visit
me to help me feel better. This led to

> **Mom's Saying 2:** They don't always have to be the *one*,
> Megan.

She said date, have fun, see what you like.

Of course, that trip, even if she had good intentions, turned sour.
My best friend on the team and I couldn't find her in the airport. She'd
had a few cocktails on the plane, and these were just the beginning days
of cell phones, so we couldn't reach her. I let her stay in my dorm room
because I knew if I left her at a hotel, she would get into way too much
trouble. Then my coach somehow found out my mother stayed in my
dorm room, and I got reprimanded for using my team's expenses to al-
low my mother to come stay and visit me. If they only knew *why*.

My next relationship was even more serious (in my head-over-heels
opinion). I was ready to permanently move to Colorado for this guy.
He even came to California to visit my parents. He even gave me a

promise ring. I'll never forget my dad's words: "What's the promise?" Guess Dad didn't see what I saw. I was a serial monogamist to boyfriends who weren't ready for my old soul, which just wanted security, a healthy home, and a healthy relationship. That breakup made me totally want to dodge town. Again, I felt like it was the end of the world. Another reason to leave Denver. No chance. I had to stay and finish school, which luckily was only one semester away.

That was really it as far as boy world went, other than a few flings that didn't go anywhere. I never really casually dated, and I hate casual sex. If I was going to sleep with you, you were going to be my boyfriend, so be ready. That made the "let's go to dinner, let's go to a movie"—all harmless gestures to get to know me—go out the door if I didn't see a promising, long-term future. Part of having an addictive personality is establishing routine that lasts, which lacks spontaneity and living in the moment.

CHAPTER 22:
Two Gal Pals

I made two really great friends in Denver who were my future brides-maids. One was a teammate, and one was someone I met through this teammate's friend. I made few friends in classes, but as far as really getting close to any of the girls on my team, I was very distant due to my socializing mistakes and basketball troubles. The girl on my team I most connected with is still my very good friend today, and she lives in New Mexico. I will say that as someone who has that out-of-sight-out-of-mind mentality, I have troubles with keeping in touch, but she is worth that effort.

The other friend, who was not on my team, was and is still my saving grace as a friend. She has been through my highs and low and understands me. I hate that going back to Denver to visit her is almost out of the question for me because I have so many negative associations, but I'm considering it. She understands and she understands that my routines also trouble me to get away. We can talk forever on the phone, we text and text, and she knows me for me. I wish I had her here in California because I don't have a friend to whom I can just say, "Hey, let's go for a walk or go to the beach." She was a solid *always* go for a walk, out to eat, anything. She lost her father not too long ago, so she has a role with her mother like I do with my dad, and we laugh and joke about our parent-children. Love you, Paige and J. Ruck.

CHAPTER 23

Figuring It Out

Photo credit Kathy Magerkurth

After college, it took me a while to figure it out. My sister had opened a dance studio, and my brother was now an attorney, so I felt a need to be something. I wanted to go down one path and start my adult life, but then I steered off into various directions. College was not the highlight of my life, and truly I'd rather cut those years out. Having a full-ride scholarship was a dream come true, but the sheltered, nonsocial life of my earlier years set me up for a multitude of troubles when I moved to Denver. Having never had much experience with boys led to a whirlwind of attention when they started looking at me. Going from having never tried alcohol to having it all around to actually drink (not just watch my mom) was a whole new element. I went from never having worn makeup to waking up fifteen minutes earlier to apply it. I was a new me in a new place, and my eyes were just now opened to what other people my age engaged in and "hung out" doing. The result was that I made plenty of mistakes. I think many adolescents got these mistakes out in high school, but as a late bloomer, I faced them head-on in college.

I went from a life of basketball being at the forefront and my purpose for waking up every day, to staying up late, scraping by on doing my homework, hardly studying for tests, and caring more about being popular than playing the sport I once obsessed over. Now playing basketball was about being the best to impress the boys and be the most popular girl on the team. I used to lose sleep over my grades, and now I just wanted to sleep. When it came time to pick a major, kinesiology was the obvious answer. Believe it or not, I didn't want to work that hard for that major. I was and still am terrible at anatomy, biology, and any sciences, so I wasn't willing at the time to put that type of energy into school. I ended up choosing criminal justice because a couple of girls on the team had this major and said it was easy. It seemed like a fast track to graduating too. It was a mistake, but I got a degree.

With that degree I asked, "Well, what now?" Of all people, I was too scared to pass a background check to become a cop. My Miss Innocent self thought that because I had drunk alcohol underage, I would not pass. Then I said, "Hey, I'll be some sort of lawyer like my brother. Better yet, I'll be a sports agent." I signed up for a few practice courses to take the LSAT and attended them at night and on the weekends. I started to regain my knack for school and did spend a great deal of time self-studying for this. I took advantage of the course's policy that if you took the two-month-long course and felt unprepared, you could take it again at no cost. Basically, my gut was telling me the LSAT wasn't going too well for me. I did make a friend in the class, and we even met to study together a few times. We both took the test on the same date, and she told me she had an extra ticket to see the band Korn. Death metal was never my forte, but I went and will never forget that venue and atmosphere.

I felt a little robbed in college that no academic adviser ever sat me down when making my schedule and asked me about what I wanted to become or do. I felt pressed to pick a major, any major, and just sort of take the right classes for it. I was very close to my high school counselor, who actually counseled me a little bit after college when I was so lost, so I felt like I had no idea where I was headed in college. Mr. Lee is the very person who wrote the forward for this book.

Having scored decently on the LSAT, I applied for a few law schools, mostly in California since I was getting the hell out of Denver. I left the day after graduation to get back to Cali. Soon I would hear back from a school and decide what was to come next. In the meantime, I moved back into my parents' house and needed to get a job of some sort. A family friend was an attorney with an office only five minutes away, so I called him up and asked if I could get a little part-time gig to get some experience under my belt and see what I thought of this whole law thing. He was the very same lawyer who helped my mom through her DUIs and helped her keep her dignity as much as possible.

My idea of being a sports agent was the glitz and glamour of going to games and being around high-profile athletes. Well, my short stint as a paralegal quickly proved that there is little interaction with actual people, lots of paperwork, and a lot of just being in an office at a desk. I worked for another attorney as well and still felt like the walls were closing in on me. Here I was again just picking a job like I picked a degree and then not really liking it. This was hard for me to swallow because I was and still am so goal oriented. Quick decisions about degrees and careers aren't exactly ideal. In my heart I knew I was not a good paralegal.

And then my application responses came back. And then, I met Carl.

Just when I thought my world was going to be over like the caterpillar, the wings of change emerged.

CHAPTER 24:
Carl Entered My Life

I graduated college in the winter of 2007. It was December and basketball season when I moved home. Dad was of course coaching, and a few things had changed with mom. It was nice seeing her, and we did go shopping *a lot*, but then there was this other observation I had made: she couldn't drive anymore. The addiction had gotten her into some run-ins with the law that I hadn't been informed of. The minivan had a device in it now that she had to blow in to check her alcohol level before driving. Well, since she was still drinking, she just opted not to drive. Then after a couple of more DUIs, she got those privileges revoked anyway. She started asking me to give her rides to whatever meetings she was going to with all types of interesting people. I figured out it was Alcoholics Anonymous after a while. Her life became *Driving Miss Daisy*.

Mom wasn't looking too great these days either. She seemed so petite and more of a skeleton of herself. It seemed like she had aged so much and was weak. Damn those sinus infections. They had really taken a toll.

My dad was a little upset with me that I moved home and didn't stay to play my senior year. The school had a new coach, and he thought I could have had a fresh start my senior year. I was beyond done. We had a little rough patch, but then he asked me to film his basketball games. I'd make a little chump change, and that was a nice side gig I had for that basketball season.

One night after a game, Dad and I went on our normal stop to get something to eat afterward. We went to a local sports bar to check out whatever NBA game was on. It was nice to be back in Oceanside, to be back with my dad, and to go to some of my favorite places I had missed the last three years. We walked in together, and right away, we heard a few voices yell, "Coach Johnson! Coach Johnson!" There was a group of about eight or ten guys, all alumni of my high school, sitting at a table. There was also one girl. They asked us to come over and join them, so we did. And there was Carl.

Want to know his first pickup line? "Wow, Megan, you have turned into such a woman." Me? Miss Size-A Chest, and hair in two French braids with a beanie on? Me? Why, thank you. When we sat down, I went next to Carl, but there was also another female on the other side of him. Who was she? Carl asked for my number, saying we should catch up and hang out. My response was, "Who is she?" He had one of those long-term relationships that slowly dwindled out as you try to mend what can't be mended in an attempt to not feel like so much time together was wasted. That's who she was, but on the other hand, she really looked like a woman compared to me. High heels, a nice trendy top, and tight jeans, hair done, makeup on point—and then there was me on the other side. Not being up for games, I gave Carl my number and said, "Well, you can see if I'm not busy sometime, and maybe we can hang out."

That night when we left and said our goodbyes in the parking lot, Carl said, "Hey, Coach Johnson, I'm going to marry your daughter." Just like that. My dad chuckled and sort of went along with the idea and then we left.

Carl started texting me. I wanted no part of it. The girl on the other side did not sit well with me, and how could I know it was really done— really, really done—between them? We played a back-and-forth game of him texting me and me saying I was busy. Then my brother was home from New York that holiday season, so we decided to throw a New Year's Eve party—one fell swoop so he could see all his friends. I invited a few people and decided it wouldn't hurt to offer the invitation to Carl. And you know he said? "I have plans." And you know who those plans were with? That girl. I found that out later.

A few weeks after the holidays died down, he texted me again. I said, "Look, I'm going to go work out at the gym and probably shoot some hoops. You can join." He showed up; we played Horse and a few flirtatious games of one on one. That's all it took. We said we wouldn't spend a night apart after that. It wasn't love at first sight, but it was damn near close to it after we actually spent time together. It was love at first hangout.

CHAPTER 25:
Don't Be That Girl

Carl and I married June 23rd for Michael Jordan

Gosh dang it, I had just met this boy, and now I had to decide if I wanted to move away again for possibly law school. But I wasn't going to be that girl who gave up her dream for some boy. The trouble was, I wasn't sure if that was my dream. College had left me with this sense of "There's more to life than basketball and school," but that world lacked the routine and structure I had always relied on. What made me even more wary was the fact that on top of my siblings having their lives set, Carl knew he wanted to be in parks and recreation for the rest of his life and was already working in the field. I felt behind the mark on my career; granted, I was only twenty-one years old. I had graduated a year early from college but felt like I was so behind on entering the real world.

I guess I have a habit of putting just a little bit of pressure on myself. In many ways it is positive pressure, but there can be a breaking point. My job with family-friend lawyer number one was only a temporary favor, so I went on good old Craigslist, found another paralegal job, and took a few months to decide whether law school was right for me. I wasn't ready because I wasn't sure. I then decided to pursue a master's in legal studies. A few months of online classes told me that was pointless. What was I going to be, a professional paralegal? That wasn't me. It was back to the chopping block of wondering, "What shall I become?" In the meantime, I started coaching basketball at the middle school level and grew fond of basketball again after such a poor college experience with it. Time sort of ticked by. I was falling in love, and my mom was getting worse and worse.

After only about three months of dating each other, Carl asked me to move in with him. At the time, it wasn't like I was thrilled to be living with my parents, but between not knowing what I was going to do for the rest of my life and then not having a whole lot of cash, the idea was tempting and scary. Like a little girl, I went upstairs to ask my mom what I should do. Now you see, she did have good advice, and no matter what anyone says, talking to your mom always makes you feel better. She was very fond of Carl from the start. She even told me not to mess this one up. Her advice was that I should try it. Go live with him, and if it didn't work out, she would let me come back. It was only ten minutes down the street, so I wasn't taking some cross-country excursion that would uproot my entire life. We moved in together.

My mom thought the world of Carl. We had gone to some type of family holiday brunch at La Costa Resort and Spa in Carlsbad,

California, and even though I had only dated Carl a short period of time, my mom told me I needed to get married there. She was paying for it, so she said that's where it would be. Five years later (too late for my mom to attend), I married Carl at that very location. Her spirit, represented by butterflies, was released by my brother during the ceremony. That monarch that stayed and watched will forever be in my heart.

Now here's a point I should bring up.... Carl is black. With the way I was raised, I'm color blind to people. A very fond memory of the whole interracial relationship was Pop Pop's response to my wedding. Traditionally, those in attendance at a wedding sit on the bride's or groom's side. That meant that black people filled one half, and my family, as Irish as ever, sat on the other side. Pop Pop asked if there was a reason black and whites were separated. The man was ninety; he'd grown up in conservative Georgia. Bless his heart.

Now, I smirk while sharing this next part. I had an unforgettable chat with my mom about Carl, which led to Mom's Saying 3. We were sitting in her bed talking, as we did from time to time because it was the only way I could spend time with her. As the topic of Carl always came up, she said the following:

Mom's Saying 3: So is it different with a black guy?

You know damn well what she was referring to, and you know damn well I wasn't going to answer that question. Shocked and amused, now with tears in my eyes from the laughter, I merely responded that a lady never tells. That was one of my favorite final talks with her.

Despite these positive memories of talks with her in that bed, I was beginning to become mad at her, with an anger and hate that raged inside of me toward her. Mind you, those talks were few and far in between the day-to-day chaos her addiction caused. She expected me to take her places, wake up early to get her to AA meetings, and cart her around whenever she needed. I was such a spoiled brat. Granted, she was paying my bills, and I was too self-absorbed to give her rides? But it wasn't my fault she was an alcoholic. I was mad that all she ever did was sleep and lie in bed, and worst of all, she could get her act together when other people came around. For my dad and me, she could not care less what she did and what she put us through. But when my brother or sister came to visit, she could brush her hair and put on an act. Harsh words, I know, but why didn't my dad and I matter enough to pretend being sober around?

We even went to her AA birthday parties, celebrating however long she had been sober. That was incredibly awkward when she was still getting hammered regularly.

Patience has never been my best quality. It takes patience to have patience, and when you have very little of it, the fuse gets short quickly. I would sit in the parking lot waiting for her to come out of a meeting, waiting for her to go into the pharmacy and come back out, just waiting and waiting. She had this habit of taking forever when going places, and that can be verified by other people. I had given up sleeping in and going for a run on a Saturday morning to take her to a meeting and then be guilted into the errands on the way home. Now it would be practically 2:00 p.m., and my day off was shot. It wasn't like I had a social life to attend to, but my addictive personality and getting all my tasks done on my schedule was nearly impossible and derailed by what was now my Grandma-Marge-taxi-driver role for her. My dad had basketball tournaments on the weekends, so who else was going to do it? She did take actual taxis a few times during the week when we couldn't take her; mind you, these were the days before Uber and Lyft. But when she did that, I felt like a jerk because she would spend all that money on those rides.

CHAPTER 26:
Guilt versus Anger

I have a lot of guilt about many things that took place. Those rides were part of it, but I have guilt for just my overall selfishness, immaturity, and constant disgust toward her. All I wanted was for her to be normal for me, not just when other people came around. I feel bad about getting physical with her. I feel bad about lying a few times and making her take a taxi. I don't like how I used to take advantage of the fact that she tried to buy my love. I feel bad that I didn't try to just spend time with her upstairs more—just lie down and watch a show with her, anything. I feel bad that we were never home. I feel bad that I took my dad's attention away from her.

However, the guilt and the anger go back and forth in my mind. I think about the time I pushed her down the stairs, but then I think about the time she whacked me across the head with her hand so hard I fell flat on my feet. I used to rip the drinks right out of her hands and pour them out into the sink. That would infuriate her. I'd just snatch it and dump it, being so pissed off at her. I did that a lot in high school when she couldn't come pick me up or come to my game, and she'd have a drink in hand in bed, watching some Lifetime movie. She chased me down the stairs and into the front yard, where I would fling those vodka bottles into the bushes. We fought like sisters all the time like that, knowing exactly how to set each other off. Guilt versus anger was the basis of my relationship with her.

CHAPTER 27:
Eye-Opening Incidents

There were three incidents I can recall that opened other people's eyes, including my sister's and brother's, to what was going on. Prior to that, until you live with an addict and are immersed in the addiction, no one can understand the immense capacity it takes over. It wasn't that my siblings were oblivious to the fact that she had a drinking problem; it was that they didn't know how bad it really was.

1. Other people: My sister had an extravagant wedding in Calabasas, California. (Home to the Kardashians, just for your information.) Open bar, of course. The mother of the bride has her duties that day and her role walking down the aisle. But my mom was too intoxicated to stand up straight and had to be held up by my foster brother to make the walk. This was the first time my aunt, my uncle, her best friends, and many of my sister's friends saw how extreme her drinking had gotten.

2. Sister: After my sister had her first child, we made a few more frequent trips than usual up to LA to visit her. I was actually there for my niece's first bath and for my sister trying to figure out how to breastfeed when we were out in public. Those were memorable times for me because I haven't had a lot of close moments in my adult life with my sister. I'm not sure how my mom got alcohol once we got to my sister's, but she drank herself into such an oblivion that she walked into the neighbor's house and passed out on their couch. That was an interesting knock on the door from my sister's neighbors, who weren't even exactly sure

who this woman was. I needed my sister to understand what was going on, and this was God's way of letting her know that life at home wasn't good for me.

I had tried to communicate the problem to my sister before, but I think she thought I was just being a normal teen who couldn't get along with her mom. In high school while my mom still had her job, she had a couple friends over who enjoyed 3:00 p.m. happy hour with her pretty frequently. Outraged that she couldn't take me to practice, I ripped the Bloody Mary from her hands and poured it down the sink. Her drinking buddy then dumped her Bloody Mary over my head, as if to stand up for my mom. That did it. I called a close family friend and asked her to take me to the train station because I needed to run away. I stayed at my sister's a few nights until the storm calmed. It was the first time I just left all my responsibilities behind. I was an elected member of the student council, and we had a huge event that week. My teacher even asked my dad where I had been because they needed me. My dad just gave a little head tilt and nod as if to say, "You know why she isn't here."

3. Brother: My brother had my niece with his girlfriend (his now wife) in New York, and they came to visit. Mom put herself together, trying to play normal. We went to Legoland. Eventually my mom wandered off, and we continued to explore the park, letting my niece have a good time. We were ready to go home and couldn't find my mom anywhere. We went back to the car, looked in bathrooms, shops, everywhere. About an hour later, we decided to just go back to the car and wait. She was passed out in the front seat. Maybe now my brother would understand what was going on.

You see, all these people who saw a glimpse of the addiction could go home concerned and surprised. But my dad and I went home and lived with it.

CHAPTER 28:
I Understood

Team mom and dad

I was a smart, good kid. I never got into trouble. I didn't have to be disciplined. But just like any teenager, I knew how to talk back and sure did to my mom. There was a point where I hated her, and I don't say the word "hate" loosely. I truly despised her. We had such a back-and-forth relationship. I would take her to AA, and we would stop on the way home and let me get my nails done or buy me an outfit. We could have such close talks upstairs in her room, and then end the day with her telling my dad what an ungrateful bitch I was. We negotiated our love and tolerance for one another. There was always a price for her to pay if she wanted me to do something for her. I didn't feel like I needed to listen to someone like her.

Meanwhile, my dad was sort of put at odds. Here I was, a good kid, and there she was, declining. It didn't matter what GPA or what sports award I got; it didn't impress my mom, and my dad wouldn't even mention it to her. If my mom told my dad to yell at me or punish me, whenever she was being authoritative toward me, my dad had to take her side. I understood. I knew that with him as a parent and husband, I would not win. This was a twisted game we played of fake parenting and acting like she didn't have a problem and was mother of the year. I understood. And much like no one else talked about the problem, neither did my dad and I. While in the car all those times or at all those dinners, he never once spoke up and told me what was really going on, and I never once spoke up and asked.

By keeping myself completely busy, I could avoid what was happening upstairs. She spent most of these years in her pajamas and would come downstairs from time to time to make a little something to eat and go back upstairs. Before everyone moved out, and when all my grandparents were still alive, my mom would be downstairs entertaining our guests and making food, but she would then disappear upstairs for long durations before returning. These were her formal years as a "functioning alcoholic," when I think my dad knew she drank a little too much, but there were no serious consequences for the issue…yet. We hosted all the holidays and family get-togethers, and eventually they did become dysfunctional. However, by that time my aunt and uncle had moved too far away to come anymore, and my grandparents were too elderly to have any sense of time. We would wait hours for the dinner to be ready, and then it would end up being takeout from somewhere anyway.

I will never truly know what pain my mother was in or what caused her to drink. Every addiction is mixed with pain. I often fear that her being a perfectionist drove her to the pain. I don't want to end up that way. I can only guess at what blows led to her drinking.

CHAPTER 29

The Blows

Hit number one was when my grandpa, her dad, died. Hit number two was when she lost her teaching job. Sometime near the end of my senior year and my first year of being at college, allegations were made that she was drinking and teaching. The fine line between being a "functioning alcoholic" and one who couldn't hold herself together was starting to come to the surface. People were noticing and not talking about it, but they were whispering about it. A formal complaint was filed. Fortunately, my mother's incredible healthy teaching years came back to help her. The principal gave her a nice medical retirement package, and this teaching chapter of her life was quickly closed. Hit number three came when she got a DUI and then another DUI, and then another, and she actually had to spend a few nights in jail.

Step one is of course seeking help. The cycle of rehabilitation began. I can remember my dad saying she was just going away for a little while getting some treatment. I still half-heartedly believed the sinus infection excuse but began to realize there was more to the story. She went to rehab for thirty or sixty days a couple of times. I can remember vising her at one of the homes, and I can also remember visiting her on a family day, which was like a giant AA meeting. The person running the meeting then had individual time with our family. He called me the "hero" of the family, which meant he labeled me as the person who tried to keep it all together for everyone, I guess. I just was the last one at home who still needed her parents.

At one point when my sister now knew what was happening, she tried to take me to Al-Anon. I was only sixteen or seventeen, and I sat there to give it a try. I just couldn't see how listening to everyone else's problems could help me. Whose sob story was worse? I didn't relate and I didn't like feeling like my sister could just go home to her normal life, and I would leave to go back to the problem. Again, when outside input tries to help those on the inside of addiction, no one can relate or understand. No one.

And then, eight months after I moved back home, and six months after I started dating Carl, it happened.

CHAPTER 30:
Purple Lips

As I was working my second attempt at becoming a paralegal, coaching middle school basketball, dating Carl, and figuring it all out *still* (okay, only like for eight months), this wasn't a bad time of my life. It just wasn't that exactness and set-in-stone feeling I wanted to have. But God truly, truly had a reason that I came home from college after year three and had this eight months' time to be at home. I wholeheartedly believe that God had me graduate college in three years for a reason.

The office where I was working as a paralegal was merely five minutes away from my parents' house. I would go to their house on my lunch breaks to make a bowl of cereal, check on my mom, and say hi to my dad if he were home from school. Although I was living with Carl just ten minutes away, I still went home all the time (daily).

It was the summer of 2008, which meant my dad was home from school for a couple of months. As usual, I came home on my break, went through their fridge, ate something, and checked in with my dad. He was enjoying summer vacation. He was downstairs reading the paper, just enjoying a slow day and time off. I asked how Mom was, and he said, "Eh, she's got a sinus infection, but you can go check on her." Typical response. I walked back into my old room to grab a sweater because I was suddenly very cold. It was summertime, so it was sort of odd to feel like I was freezing, but I do run cold. One of my two best friends from Colorado called to say hi, knowing it was about that time for my lunch break. But I told her that for some reason I was really cold and didn't feel well. I said, "Let me talk to you later." I looked in the mirror, and my lips were *purple*.

We hung up and I sort of shook off the cold chill. I needed to get back to work but hadn't made it upstairs to see my mom yet. I walked upstairs, expecting her to be lying in bed. She wasn't there. So I went to the bathroom to see if she was in there. And she was—lying face down on the bathroom floor, wearing a long skirt but naked from the waist up. I froze. "Mom, are you okay? Mom?" I was frozen. I squatted down beside her, placed my hand on her bare back, and waited for it to rise and fall with her breathing. Nothing.

Running downstairs, I screamed, "Dad, Mom isn't breathing. She's not breathing!" He popped up from the recliner, told me to call 911, and raced upstairs. I grabbed the house phone, called, and ran back up. My dad had turned my mom over on her back. And then I saw her, jaundiced and purple in the face, mouth and eyes open. The operator told me to put my dad on speaker and for him to start CPR. He was trying and trying. The ambulances raced up our cul-de-sac, and I let them in; the paramedics quickly followed me upstairs. It was fast, it was hectic, and it was loud. Amid this chaos, my dad and I looked at each other, thinking there's just no way she's going come back to life.

I went back downstairs, called my sister, and said, "I think Mom is dead." In disbelief she wasn't registering or processing this, so as I paced all around and went outside for air, I yelled on the phone, "I think Mom is dead!" My dad had come back downstairs and said that was it. I confirmed the information to my sister. That was it. I had found my mom's corpse on the bathroom floor, and that was it. The cold. I felt her death. The autopsy revealed she had suffered a stroke after an abrasion to the head. Lost her damn balance and fell. Simple but so final. Her cold and lonely light just couldn't shine anymore.

My brother was called right away, and somehow our closest friends came to the house immediately. I called my boss since technically I was on my lunch break, and he came to the house too. The rush. The finality. And then the *what now?* A mother is the glue of the family, sick or not. Irreplaceable. The figure whom we all believe to be indestructible. It didn't matter that she was an alcoholic anymore. She was my mother.

And then there was Carl and me. What now? What could he say? He was one of the first people on scene. We were young and freshly together. He just left work and came. And people kept coming. Despite the outpouring of love, no one ever asked how or why. No one ever addressed the secret. They just stood by my family.

CHAPTER 31:
Blame

Photo credit Alex Castro

Having said and shared all this, I'd take my mom back in a heartbeat, addiction and all. She is forever present in my life, every single day, even as the years pass on. I don't blame her for wanting to escape, I don't blame her for not being able to be a fully functioning parent, and I don't blame her for the countless disappointments I encountered with her. I *do blame* her for my driven, ambitious nature, my perfectionist attributes, my love for education, my love of shopping and coordinating outfits, and my love of performing and being on stage. All the good qualities that make me who I am—these are what I *blame* her for. The experience of addiction and its power has taught me to know my strengths and weaknesses and play to them accordingly.

As the child of an addict, I don't do anything in moderation. It's all or nothing. When I play, I play to win and be the game changer. I'm going to be the star. When my mind is set, it's set. As much exercise is part of my life, it is an addiction. I physically and mentally crave it, and I have withdrawal without it. I put it before many other things and can be very selfish about my day until the exercise part is complete. Let's say I'm doing the elliptical for twenty minutes. Eventually that twenty minutes turns into thirty, and then forty, and then an hour, and so on. It's like my tolerance has grown, so I keep needing more and more. There are certainly worse things in life to be addicted to, but when something becomes overblown, there are consequences to pay.

I tire myself out and feel a need to do so. Every repetition and set counts. If somehow there is a disruption to that, then that means I *have to* finish later. Staying late and taking longer than necessary has been a fallback for me many times. That means the schedule has been changed, and it makes the upcoming tasks thrown off their course. It's a problem for an inflexible person. *Time* is the dictator, and when every single item has to be checked off, those twenty-four hours in a day are productively used, each and every second. Again, that means no time for socialization, chats on the phone with a girlfriend, or just watching TV. I'm a tough act to follow and tough to be around at times. My closest allies know that there's a time and place for them, which sounds selfish (and is), but that's Megan.

It's as if I constantly ask myself, "What's next?" Exercise has been my escape.

> *You can be addicted to alcohol but really the addiction is to escaping reality.*
>
> —Anonymous

CHAPTER 32:
I'm Still Standing

Photo credit Kathy Magerkurth
Take a close look...there's a butterfly in the background

Twelve years later, I'm still standing after all these years. The image of that day never ceases to exist. It can be haunting, but it isn't a vision that causes me agony or pain anymore. I have come to terms that God wanted my mother to be happy, pain free. She is with God, her parents, and her relatives; she could be in no better place and is at peace. This life on earth was no longer tolerable or worth living for her.

I always speak of quality of life with my clients, and when that no longer is part of your day to day, then change has to take place.

Alcoholism is a disease. My mother did not choose to be isolated, depressed, or jobless or to spend her time in bed. The disease made her powerless. When she was able to attend rehab for thirty, sixty, or however many days, she came back with a vengeance each time. When she came home, I'd have thoughts and spurts of a mother, of someone I longed for who had color in her face, a zest for living, and a spirit that had seemed to be mended. But each time, that was short lived. The disease knocked on her door every waking minute, and finally her fight just wasn't enough.

Guilt. Guilt made her drink again. Imagine being sober and thinking about the job you lost, the parenting you hadn't done, the absent wife you were, the friends who never called you anymore, and the list went on and on. There were no distractions from these thoughts. She wasn't working and couldn't drive, so in between AA meetings, there was time to sit and just be with herself. When your demons keep taunting you, eventually they get louder and louder. That's when all of life's problems come crashing down, and drinking makes that pain go away.

That was what drinking did for my mom: it made the pain go away. Self-medication. Quick fix, easy out. In my darkest moments, I've more than understood and related to her solution. I've wished I had an out. I've wished I could just check out, not feel, not be wrapped up in my own anxiety-ridden thoughts. But my all-natural life makes that impossible. I feel. That feeling has caused me a lot of grief. I'm more than aware of my addictive patterns and behaviors, so turning to substances would not be an option for me. Nothing in moderation. Let's say I attempted to have a nightly glass of wine. That means every night, the pattern must repeat. One nightly glass of wine would turn into slipping a second glass in, and then the next night I'd do the same, and then more and more would continue. Living in excess leads to a breaking point, and time and time again, I do that to myself. How far can I go before crashing? Luckily, I don't burn out because I reel it in just in the nick of time.

CHAPTER 33:
I Figured It Out

Photo credit Alex Castro

After my mom passed, my dad asked Carl and me to move into the house with him. Sure thing. Part of this agreement of no rent and taking care of everything for him was that I was going to go back to school. I didn't want to be a paralegal or a sports agent, but I did like coaching basketball, and I did love working out. My parents were teachers, and I had this habit of doing what people in my family did (like trying to go to law school after my brother). I decided to get my teaching credential and master's degree. My subject matter was going to be physical education. I was also going to add a credential in health. I did an online program at National University so that I could try to substitute teach and make money as well as coach basketball. Paying no rent was in exchange for me paying for my schooling.

They say when it comes to jobs, it's all about who you know. My parents were both teachers, so I had a lot of connections to the school districts. The advice of others was that if I coached, I'd be more of an asset to a school, and this would help me land a job. The educational budget has been in disarray in California for some time. I had chosen a subject matter with jobs that rarely popped up and from which many teachers waited longer to retire. When I did my student teaching, I was hired as the girls' head basketball coach at only age twenty-two. I looked like I was still in high school, but this was a big step and a big connection to landing a teaching job. That teaching job never came the following school year, so I looked around for other options. I then became the head coach at another high school that promised me a job the next year. They made me the on-site substitute teacher, which meant I potentially had a subbing job every day. I didn't, and I didn't get a job the following year as a teacher. Enrollment was too low, and they weren't adding PE—it was more like they were subtracting it.

I tried again, thinking the third time was a charm. This time I got a long-term PE job at a middle school. A teacher went on a leave of absence, so I rode it out as long as I could. Every day after work, I would go to the local corporate gym and work out for hours on end. I was off work in the early afternoon and Carl wouldn't be home until the evening, so I stayed at the gym every minute I could. One day, the manager came up to me and said it seemed like I really knew what I was doing and complimented me on my fitness level. Oddly enough, he was recruiting me to be a trainer. Little did he know, I had finished my master's degree in PE and health. He told me I needed to get certified, and the most reputable training company's test was very rigorous. No one ever passed on the first try. I looked up when the test was being held. It was in two weeks. I had the book overnighted, read it, took the test, passed it, and then brought him the results. Surprised, he said, "When can you start?" I gave my two-week notice at the subbing job, with my gut telling me teaching wasn't on the horizon.

Working as a corporate trainer, I hustled. I was the top female salesperson and impressed everyone at the location. I was top dog. After a while, the hustle was wearing me out for minimum wage. Carl got a job with an hour's commute, and we decided we should move that way. I wanted to give teaching another go, considering this would be in a new school district. The subbing game started again, but it became another hopeless quest of false promises. I then interviewed and was rehired at the corporate gym down in this area.

I have always loved taking group exercise classes. In between training clients, I would go to the classes to get my workouts in. Then I thought, "I could totally teach these!" I obtained one certification after another...cycle, Zumba, yoga, water aerobics, boot camp. All of them. I fell in love teaching these classes and training people. Yet here I was, working very hard for very little money with my master's degree. It was frustrating and I wasn't sure long term where this job would take me. I wasn't getting health insurance or retirement, but I liked what I was doing. Long term is what I always wanted with everything.

CHAPTER 34:
Yoga

I had a pretty full repertoire of certifications at this point, but the gym needed another yoga instructor. They asked me to attend a certification the weekend coming up, but that was the service date we planned to spread my mom's, Grandma Marge's, and Bernard's ashes together. Sadly, Grandma Marge did pass a few years after my Mom. The corporate world, as it is, said, "Well, go the weekend after, but it's in Merced, California." Merced? Where was that? Oh, just seven hours away. Sure, let me get a hotel on my minimum-wage pay and drive there. I told Carl; he said, "Let's roll." He had a rental car because his car was in the shop, and he figured a weekend playing video games in a hotel room wasn't too bad.

The workshop was at a small, private training studio in downtown Merced. There was a group of seven or eight of us, so it was an intimate environment and a really great program. As I got to know the other attendees, the girl who owned the studio was getting certified too. She has inquired about my current work status and experience and was shocked I was doing what I was doing. She said I was overqualified, underpaid, and not living up to my potential. I said I had no idea how she made it having her own business and location. A couple of tips and suggestions, and my thoughts were scrambling.

The drive home from Merced, of all places, was life changing. I turned to Carl and said that I wanted to open my own fitness studio. Never one to compromise my goals, he said, "Okay, well, how are you going to do that?" I said I'd use some of my Grandma Marge inheritance. He asked where. I said Oceanside, because that was our community. He agreed we should move back to our city and he would commute to San Diego. He asked what I wanted to call it. Like we were picking baby names, we came up with Every BODY's Fit.

The very next day, Monday, I looked up places to rent and businesses to buy. I found an old karate studio in Oceanside and set up an appointment with the landlord. We met on Tuesday. I had no credit to my name, so he asked for a cosigner. I said my dad would (I hadn't asked but knew he would). I explained my vision, and he just said, "You know what? I'll give you a year. You look like a girl with a dream." I was a studio owner.

The first six months consisted of cleaning and cleaning to pass the time and hoping someone would walk through the door. I didn't have much in the account to advertise anymore, so I made some really nice flyers and decided to walk door to door to distribute them. The postal service expense to do this was far out of my price range, so I did it. Sunburned and tired, I walked from morning until dark for three days. That is how I found all the hills around my studio that I walk or run with clients during training sessions. People even ask if I chose my location for the hills, but no—they just turned out to be my signature warm-up.

Hard work has always been my strong suit. I have been blessed to help change so many lives through movement. I figured out how I could help people best. I went from tapping my pen on the desk, begging for clients, to working twelve-hour days. It is the most rewarding job ever. I love it, but I worry and worry about the highs and lows of how a business works. Not easy for an anxiety-ridden gal. Sales is part of the profession.

Over the past seven years, I have obtained many other certifications, I've been featured in business and fitness magazines, and I'm always trying to get as much exposure as I can. I've been on the local news a few times, I've been nominated for some pretty prestigious awards like the AAU Sullivan Award, which Michelle Kwan and Michael Phelps have won, and my trophies line the walls of the studio. I bring my pug, Steve Nash (basketball, of course), to work as the mascot. He has a neat YouTube channel of workouts he does with me. My other pug, Phil Jackson, is elderly and hangs with my dad at home. I bought a house walking distance from my studio two years ago. It only took two weeks for my dad to decide he didn't want to live alone. His overnight stay is now permanent. I wouldn't have it any other way. My two favorite people and my pugs are my home.

I have had the pleasure of writing articles for magazines and newspapers. I have earned the highest accreditations. Then two years ago, I decided to step my game up even more and get my doctorate.

I was a speaker at a training conference, and afterward I decided to walk around the exposition. There was a booth of a school that offered a program, and I was interested right away. I asked them to follow up with me in a few days. Unfortunately, I missed the application deadline, having met the recruiter after the date, so that fueled my fire to find another school. I applied in October and started in January 2018. Soon I will have my doctorate in health and human performance from Concordia University. It has been a challenging feat for sure, but I actually look forward to each course and the assignments. The go-getter than I am, I usually power through the first four weeks of each eight-week class and try to get my work all done. That way, the remaining four weeks, I'm more freed up for writing, whatever comes my way with the studio, and photo shoots.

I plan to write my dissertation on a program I have designed called PAIPAA, the Physical Activity Intervention Program for Alcohol Addiction. Exercise is medicine and can be used as a coping mechanism and alternative to alcohol use. Most rehabilitation centers do not offer exercise beyond free hours in the day, when residents could use what minimal equipment is available or walk. My intention is to help addicts find a different way to obtain the pleasures of positive endorphins and to feel the physical and mental improvements to quality of life that exercise can offer. This would be a thirty-day program offered at recovery centers that would initiate the habitual use of exercise posttreatment for residents.

I have helped many people in my studio, and I'm sure if the walls could talk, they would have many stories to share about tears, fears, and accomplishments. A few clients have exceeded losing over one hundred pounds. Many have gotten off or lowered their medications for high blood pressure, high cholesterol, and diabetes. Thousands and thousands of inches have been lost off many bodies. Many pounds have disappeared. Lives have been changed through movement, which is what I set out to do. I believe that every BODY is fit, and every exercise is possible for any body type, given the appropriate modifications and accommodations. I've had people over age seventy doing burpees, so where there is a will there is a way, and I can confidently say I know way to make it possible.

CHAPTER 35:
My Alcohol Intake...or Lack Thereof

When I did drink in college, before age twenty-one, I took it too far immediately. I had only been at school a few months, tried to fit in and no one knew my homelife, so I drank and acted like this wasn't my introduction to it. Silly me, thinking I could be normal and have a few drinks with the girls and go out dancing. New to the scene and never having lived in moderation, I drank myself to the point I ended up in the emergency room. I had to have my stomach pumped. My best friend on the team phoned dad for me. My daddy's girl image he had of me would be tarnished. When I called him the next day, he told me, "If you ever end up like your mother, I will never speak to you again." That ended college drinking for me.

I tried to drink when I first returned from college. Our society is so enthralled with drinking, especially now with all the breweries. It is a constant in-your-face beverage. Beer has always been distasteful to me, so I tried to do the ladylike thing and have wine. I was just drinking to fit in, not because I liked it. When you first date someone, they order a drink for you, but soon Carl learned it wasn't my style. God's protective nature for me was that I never had a taste for the popular options. That left fruity-tooty drinks, but always being mindful of my waistline, I never wanted to go that route.

When I did have those glasses of wine, I felt terrible about drinking, knowing all that this liquid had done to destroy a person and part of my life. Not worth it. There was also an incident that flares up an image when I tried to drink. Some family friends and part of my family went to a Mexican restaurant one evening, and because I had turned twenty-one, I ordered a margarita along with everyone else (except mom, who was in her attempting phase number five hundred of trying not to drink). She flashed me a look that could kill. How could I dare order a drink when she could not? It was me shoving it right back in her face. Yeah, I ordered it out of spite, but I never drank it.

Therein lies one of the conundrums I'll never understand about the people in my mom's life. Adults who absolutely knew her problem (and didn't talk about), continued to drink in front of her and with her. As much as it hurts to admit, why did my dad never stop drinking? Why was alcohol so important or powerful to others that they couldn't give it up? How in the world was it that hard to go out to eat and not have a cocktail? How could we continue to host holidays (although always dramatic now) and have the cooler stocked with alcohol? Not that everyone had to share in the problem, and it wasn't anyone else's problem, but it seemed unreal to me that alcohol couldn't be spared or eliminated.

In my adult life, I clearly have negative associations with alcohol. I can be around it. I can go to bars. But my tolerance for what it does and can do is very little. Don't ask me for a ride because you have had too many drinks. I lived a lifetime of giving rides to an alcoholic. Don't expect me to wait for you to have one more. I lived a lifetime of waiting for rides and waiting for AA meetings to be over. Don't expect me to stop on the way home to grab more beer for you. For someone who doesn't drink, I feel that going into a liquor store is totally strange. My sympathy and empathy just aren't there when it comes to booze, and once those around me start acting drunk, I'm done. I can laugh it off at first, but then I'm just ready to leave. When everyone else's night starts to elevate the more their alcohol goggles set in, my night has stayed the same. My sense of time and whereabouts is all there and real. When you start acting different, I'm ready to roll.

I have felt that sometimes people have the perception that because I leave early or hardly stay places, that I'm too good, too busy, or just socially uncomfortable. It really is none of those; it is more so that as other people drink and eat, their experience escalates. They get a little buzz, get a little second wind from eating, and then I'm there, just sort of hanging out on the sidelines. I don't ever feel engaged when I go places. This also includes eating. I choose to eat the way I eat, and that can be isolating, and of course I choose to not have alcohol. Between these two factors in our American culture, there isn't much room left for social outings. It doesn't make me out to be high and mighty, like I'm better than everyone else, but it separates me.

CHAPTER 36:
No Moderation

A fter all this time, people still keep asking me if I want some or if I will have some. This girl isn't going to change, and there are no exceptions for occasions because once the door opens to a person with an addictive personality, the floodgates have been let loose. Here's a little background on that: I have always eaten healthily. My mom and dad were the type that used ground turkey, never red meat; we had sugar-free vanilla ice cream in the freezer, and we always had fresh fruits and vegetables. I never had a steak until just last year. As a result, I'd come home from school and have carrots. Here's the catch: it wasn't like I was having ten carrots. I was having ten, ten, ten, and ten more, and then the bag was gone. The bottom of my feet would turn orange. It was the same concept with almonds, apricots, bowls of cereal with vanilla soy milk. Healthy foods compared to the fruit roll-ups and milk and cookies my friends were having. However, there is that token saying: everything is okay in moderation. Remember my problem with moderation? If I can't hone it on some carrots, alcohol has no standing chance.

That transcends into how I eat now. I follow a meal plan—yes, because I'm a bodybuilder, but also because of my moderation issue. Left to my own devices, as nutrition smart as I am, without accountability, I can eat anything in excess at any time. Let's say I'm going to have some ground turkey, one of my favorite proteins. Three to four ounces would be a single serving for a gal of my stature, but I can eat the entire package. Meal prep, left to my own plan, means okay, maybe a little more than four ounces...well, maybe just a little more than that, and this holds true for brown rice, sweet potatoes, you name it. I eat until I'm fully full and uncomfortably full.

That is why I need to answer to someone else for a meal plan. As a coach's daughter, it registers guilt to me if I don't do what I'm told. I listen. Going back to others offering me food or beverages, the answer has to be no for me, or else I will continue to eat what they offer and continue to drink what they offer. I can eat and drink someone out of their house, football player style.

This addictive quality transcends to working out too. Left on my own, I can go for hours on end. Ride the elliptical? Sure, let's say forty-five minutes. Well, I get fixated on numbers, so it turns into sixty minutes and then maybe seventy-five minutes. The number is never satisfying. I also get caught up in making sure that I did everything. I'm supposed to do five sets. Well, on the fifth set I might question, "Was that five or four?" I have no self-trust, so I do an extra and an extra to be sure it was completed. It is better for me to work out in the confines of a group that is one hour long or with my coach in a one-hour session. When I was a trainer in the corporate world and when I was substitute teaching, I would go to the gym before and after work. I'd keep having to set my alarm earlier and earlier to maintain the add-ons I had created, and then when I would stay after work, if I knew Carl wasn't home for a while, well, that meant to keep going. There's nothing wrong with eating healthily and working out, but even those activities when not controlled in moderation can get out of hand and somehow lose their "healthy" intention.

Like the Energizer bunny, I go until there's just nothing left in the tank. I literally wear myself out daily until it is time to hit the pillow. I won't stay up extra late to finish anything, but I will get up extra-early to do something. Again, time is the ruler of many facets of life when you have an addictive personality. Resting and relaxing or having a "day off" causes too much turmoil from routine, which leads to a guilty conscience about taking a break. It's better to just wake up early and not enjoy sleeping in because then I will just think about what I didn't do all day. The restless anxiousness overshadows any sense of enjoyment anyway.

CHAPTER 37:
Eating Out and Portion Distortion

Most would never believe that I grew up primarily eating out. Fast food was a regular and prominent part of my diet. In fact, the majority of my eating was takeout. That was the result of two working parents and three kids who had activities every night. Even with Grandma Marge, we were eating out. We weren't the family that sat down for dinner every night at 6:00 p.m. When all of us were living at home, we all had practices, rehearsals, games, you name it. We had lots of McDonald's, Popeye's, Round Table, and Del Taco. Every week we had food from one of these stops at least once. Those were staples. I was beyond active, so my metabolism and youth certainly were in my favor. After my brother and sister moved out and it was my dad and I practically living on our own, we readily ate out, but now mainly at restaurants. After whatever basketball practice we were at, it would be about 7:00 p.m., and we would go to a restaurant near our location. My typical order, no matter where we were, was chicken tenders, fries, and a shake. Dad would have chicken something and a few beers.

On Sundays after my extra self-practice, my dad and I would go to the grocery store and stock up on what I wanted to make my lunch for the week ahead. I chose healthy options. I made turkey sandwiches and packed fruits. I just ate a lot of the same over and over, which has been in my favor. I don't get tired of the same, which is part of my routine nature. I've never needed variety because I thrive on routine and structure. I needed five lunches per week, so I'd buy five of whatever I wanted, such as five bananas, five yogurts, and so forth. If I knew I had a tournament that weekend, I'd buy extra snacks so that I would have those for the day. I was a really organized kid who took responsibility for making sure I had what I needed.

In college, I kept up the habit of trying to eat healthier. Living in the dorms, we had an all-you-can-eat buffet available. I had a hard time because pizzas and pastas weren't the healthier choices I wanted to make. I've been well aware of my lack of self-control when it comes to portion control. All-you-can-eat pizza? I don't know many people who stop at one or two slices when the plethora of food basically taunts you to keep going back for more.

For the first few months in college, I tried to rein it in, but I did pack on a few pounds with this freedom, with no limitation to how much I could have, especially the soft-serve ice cream. I called my mom, who I knew would understand, and said that I needed to buy my own groceries and eat more in my room than downstairs at the chow hall. I was passing up free food and asking for money for food, but she said yes. With the money I did get, I packed better lunches for myself and wanted to try to lose some of the weight I had gained. At that time, I had a false perception of what healthy was but was still eating healthier than the dorm food options. For example, I'd have a Gatorade and huge baggie of trail mix for a snack. Sugar and fat mainly, but to me, as many would assume, I was an athlete who needed the sports drink. And isn't trail mix good for you?

During college, I was actually less active than in high school. I was a three-sport athlete in high school (basketball, cross country, and track), sometimes going from one sport to another in the same day. In college, we practiced a couple of hours a day, but we ate more than we moved. When we took road trips to games, we ate before the game, having a hearty mashed potato and fried chicken meal, and then we got back on the bus after the game to be welcomed with boxes of pizza we passed around. This was topped off with each of us being given a snack pack with peanut butter and jelly sandwiches and cookies. When you think about the amount of movement that actually went on in, say, that ninety-minute game (if you even played the whole game), the rest of the day was filled sitting on the bus and waiting around for the game to start. I never went hungry in college; that was for sure.

Another part of my addictive, no moderation lifestyle is that I finish whatever I start or do. This means that, no matter what portion is in front of me, I will eat it all. So let's say after the game, I've had a few slices of pizza and I really don't need the PB&J and cookies they have given. The trouble for me is that if it's there, and as much as I might try to delay having it, I won't stop thinking about having it until I just cave in. I try to justify the calories, thinking they won't hurt me. I've never had the capability to eat half and save the other half for later. I'm an all-or-nothing, all-at-once type of gal.

CHAPTER 38:
All or Nothing

Photo credit Kathy Magerkurth

The same goes for exercise. If I start a workout, I have to finish all of it, every rep and set. Sometimes I go beyond what was the original plan. More, more, more, go, go, go. Don't settle and don't stop until you absolutely have to. Having to stop might be because I have to go somewhere or have to be somewhere, creating a time constraint, but I will squeeze in every last second on that cardio machine and every last rep that I can.

I've been fortunate that my addictions are to healthier objects and habits, nothing that has ever caused me harm. But the life of an addict is one that continues to build tolerance to whatever it is they are doing. I had reached a point where forty-five minutes on the elliptical was just a mere scratch on the surface of making myself tired or feeling like I had worked out. If you saw my closet with over a hundred pairs of shoes and all the leggings and tops I have, more and more and more is exactly what I crave in all aspects. There are a pair of shoes, earrings, a top, leggings, a necklace, Fitbit strap, and a few bracelets for every occasion that coordinate and match. I literally can never have enough. Luckily this addiction is to thrift-store shopping and getting the best bargain for these items. Lord knows, if I needed brand names and high-end clothes, I would shop myself out of house and home.

CHAPTER 39:
Friends Forever

We meet many different people throughout our lives via school, work, activities, and then throughout networks and connections. We have acquaintances, coworkers, teammates, classmates, roommates, neighbors—the list goes on and on. Part of my lack of socializing is my addictive need for permanence. Just like casual dating, I don't do casual hangouts and friendships. To me, a friend becomes a lifelong friend, not just a "we went to the beach a few times" or "we had lunch a few times" friend. To me, that's wasted time that I've spent away from my purposes and instead invested in someone else. Living near Camp Pendleton, I'm always baffled but thankful at how our service members can make friends with people from all over our country, but then they move around and leave. Temporary arrangements. Temporary encounters. I don't do temporary. So my circle is small because I'm selective about who I give my time to because I want that time to be valued and ongoing. I'm loyal to those who are loyal to me. I'm the best customer because you know I'm a lifer once I start coming, be it hair, nails, eyelashes, tanning, the works.

I don't do casual barbecues, baby showers, or birthday parties. Temporariness makes an addictive personality unable to compartmentalize just going to have fun or to meet new people. Many times, I end up attending functions to avoid being socially rude when invited. No matter the occasion, I only stay a short time because I'm completely out of my comfort zone, and my feathers are all ruffled by the wrench in my schedule.

When I first starting dating Carl, that is where we had some growing pains. He had gone to college in San Diego, so he had many people still in the area whom he was in touch with because he never left. Mind you, I was not left with the biggest circle of friends to return to when I moved back, but I had many acquaintances. I was popular by default in high school because I was good at basketball, smart in school, and just got along with everyone. I didn't have drama, and I didn't gossip. I was even on prom court senior year (the only reason I went to that one school dance).

Senior Prom with my sash, mom fell and was using a walker at the time

Carl has a vivacious personality that lights up a room and draws people in. Wherever we go, he makes friends, even across the world like in South Korea and Australia. We actually met a couple in Australia who invited us over for a family dinner because Carl met them at the bar, and they had such a great time together. When we first starting dating, he could have gone out every night with a different set of acquaintances for happy hour. At first, he did, never turning down an invitation. New to a relationship, I was being treated like the person he went to go see after he saw an old friend or hung out with whomever. Trying to avoid being too needy at first, I would go work out and get errands done after work and then wait for his text or call that he was heading over. Then I had to say something about acquaintances versus real friends.

Here we were, starting a fresh relationship, and I was being treated second to acquaintances. I explained that five or six months down the road, would these people still be around or just here and there? When life hits the fan, could you call any of them and ask for help or know that they will be there for you? I'd say he got the message and did change those habits. I felt like the boring side chick who didn't drink or really like to go out. I was the perfect girlfriend and still tell him I'm the perfect wife. You know I'm either one of a few places: at the gym, doing homework, writing, getting my eyelashes and nails done, getting a spray tan or body wrap, or thrift-store shopping. All harmless and routine. I'm easy to trust. This means at first, he could go to happy hour wherever, whenever, with people I didn't even know, and then call me when he was done.

Carl has an eye disease called keratoconus, and when he had to have a full cornea transplant, that is when the message really hit home about acquaintances versus real friends. Carl's two best friends were there, and all those "happy-hour homies," as I like to call them, never even asked how he was. He changed from being the yes man to the homebody man I have today. On the flip side, Carl has taught me about the value of family and that they are always the ones who are there for you at the end of the day. Being one of seven siblings, he really stood by being there for each one when they needed him. Meanwhile, my relationships were and still are a little sparse with my siblings. I go back and forth wanting to be a better sister and wanting to be a better aunt, but I don't know how because all my addictive behaviors don't make the space for this. My brother is in New York, and my sister is in LA, which makes the idea of seeing them even more dauting due to distance.

Among my relationships and interactions with people, I really do have an "out of sight, out of mind" mentality. When you don't come around anymore, if you left my life, I probably won't keep in touch. You have now become temporary. You don't fit into the addictive space anymore because now I have to clear space to see you. I don't do hanging out. Sometimes we might text or email and mention getting together, but I only go along with the conversation, knowing that won't happen.

In many ways, I feel like I'm that stable person, like the childhood home that my parents had. People think they will always know where to find me and I'm the strong gal who will be right where they left me. Some see me as a business entity, not a person, when in fact, I actually do have feelings and emotions. When you have an addictive personality, life is all or nothing. So again, out of sight, out of mind. You either are all in or all out in my world. Nothing personal—it's just that cut and dried.

CHAPTER 40:
Why Bodybuilding?

Photo credit Daryl Lane

Because I have always been fit and exercise driven, the clients at my studio would constantly ask me if I ever had done bodybuilding or wanted to. I hadn't and the reason had to do with supplements, but I never wanted to respond with that answer. I would just say I don't really know if steroids or that whole entity is something I want to explore.

Like most, I associated bodybuilding with Arnold Schwarzenegger and people with veins popping out of their foreheads. Although I've never tried steroids, I had been addicted to over-the-counter fat burners. This started in college when I had gained weight after the ACL injury. Being so desperate, I went to the pharmacy store and picked one off the shelf, believing what the label read that claimed I could lose weight faster. The addict in me thought that if this was the case, then I should take a few of them to expedite the results. Now all the money my mom was sending me for healthy food was being spent on different supplements that I was so vulnerable to taking because I just wanted to be skinny.

The habit continued after I graduated and moved home. I still had my bag of pills I took everywhere with me. I timed out vitamins and fat burners, and I was taking whatever was the latest promising fix. Okay, so here again, I was addicted to something seemingly healthy but taking it too far. It started with multivitamins, taking three or four types in a day because I figured the more the better, the more the healthier. Then I figured I should probably take extra of all of these for maximum, faster results. Maybe ten pills a day at this point.

Then when I became a trainer and was around trainers, who took many different supplements and were bodybuilders, I caught onto fat burners again but now the type that were a little more serious. I was going to the nutrition store now, not just the pharmacy, so my intake was growing and growing. Now nearly fifteen pills deep a day, multiple times a day, I literally had my pill purse on my sleeve with my regular purse, no matter where I went. I wasn't making tons of money, but I had to keep up with the supplement regimen. Addicts know when excess is occurring, but the mind justifies and reassures that you are in total control. I did this for a few years. Mind you, no one in my family or around me ever asked about that pill bag.

The pill popping continued into the first few years that I had my studio. So now when clients and those around me were asking why I didn't try to compete as a bodybuilder, I sort of swallowed hard, knowing that if I did that, I might get into more supplements, like steroids and performance enhancers. It was Christmastime 2015, and the idea of bodybuilding was in my mind, but that was a double-edged sword. I messaged an old trainer coworker from the corporate gym and asked him how he got into bodybuilding and what websites I might take a peek at. He told me he only did natural bodybuilding. I was like, "Natural? What does that mean?" You get drug tested; there are no supplements. You just work out and eat right.

My first thought was, "Um, I would have to stop taking all my supplements. Could I do that? Maybe this was the perfect escape from them." That friend said he would help me and coach me, so that December, I said this could be one of those trendy, cliché New Year's resolutions. I was in. My liver was ready too.

Cold turkey, I cut out the supplements, all those silly multi-multivitamins, but more importantly, the different fat burners that were causing me irritability and nausea. It was freeing. As far as the eating plan went, for the first time, I was eating in proportion. I was weighing food and sticking to ounces and grams. My body responded. At first, I lost quite a bit of weight. I was just above one hundred pounds. Some people were concerned, saying I even looked too thin and emaciated in the face. Little did they know I was detoxing and eating the right quantities, so no wonder this was happening.

My first show was in March 2016. It was at a local casino, so my clients and family filled the audience. I must have drastically increased ticket sales. I got third place, not bad. Granted, my clients and myself weren't exactly sure why, but looking at the photos, I smile at my novice posing technique. It needed work, which was critical, despite having a good-looking physique. My second show was just two weeks later. Most competitors try to line up the events to not have to diet down over and over. Well, this time, I got first place. First place, hmm, second show, hmm. Well, at this particular show, first place meant professional qualification. Seemed like I was onto something, now being named a pro, so I continued. The next local show was in November, so why not? It was my third show ever, and I was competing with the pros. I got second. After that show, the promoter approached me and told me about a competition in Italy next summer that he thought I would be a good candidate for. Me? Carl was next to me, so I turned to him. We were both intrigued by the idea. Carl answered for me: "We will go."

Well, now I needed to step my game up a little bit. Being a coach's daughter (gosh, I say that a lot), the concept of having an in-person coach, not just my friend online, was a good idea to me. That is when I started working with my current coach. A man of few words, he quickly saw my tenacity, work ethic, drive, and loyalty. I was learning how to properly pose and really taking my workouts to the next level having someone direct me. It is human nature; we work out harder when someone else like a coach or other people are around.

The summer of 2017, Carl, my dad, and I went to Rimini, Italy. Heading to the world championships on Team USA was such an incredible feeling. I had a red suit made to represent our country, and I was as excited and nervous as ever. Mainly I was scared because I was competing but also because this was my first time Carl or I had every traveled out of the country. We all three had to get passports, which was the start to the adventure, trying to figure out how that worked. The trip was well worth it, as I placed fourth...in the world. The classic American blonde on stage, I felt proud and satisfied. After the show, we explored Italy all over. From the Colosseum to the Vatican, we did that get-on-the-bus tourist thing and went for it. Absolutely amazing. Italy was more than I ever expected. The travel bug set in, and the competition road was in full swing.

CHAPTER 41:
Onward and Upward Competing

Photo credit Daryl Lane

After gaining credibility competing, I was named and still hold the title of the athlete representative for the Amateur Athletic Union (AAU). Life had come full circle because I grew up playing AAU basketball. In fact, it was AAU basketball that helped me get my college scholarship.

Most of the shows are held in Las Vegas or Laughlin. From Oceanside, this is about a five- or six-hour drive and a little weekend get-away. "Vegas, baby!" has been the routine a few times a year now. Then my coach presented the opportunity that there was an up-and-coming organization that had asked if I wanted to come compete in South Korea. Of all places in the world, I kind of thought, "South Korea?" Well, Italy was a hell of a trip, why not? I had to ask Carl first, but of course he was up for the gig. And what a trip that turned out to be. I did very well, placed high, and did my sports model basketball routine in front of a standing-room-only audience. The sports model category for AAU involves showing your sports talent and then saying a short speech after about how the sport has influenced your life. I hadn't bounced a ball in years, but just like riding a bike, it did come back quickly. After the South Korea show, the promoter and his assistant took me, Carl, and my coach all around the city. The endless Korean barbecue and great company made the trip worth every penny.

Now, as we were the newly titled "world travelers," my South Korea performance qualified me to attend the world championships, but this time in Queensland, Australia. No questions asked, we were going. South Korea was in May 2018, and Australia was in October 2018. In between this time, I made a couple of Vegas trips. I just kept going on the competition ride. I was getting the hang of hard workouts with heavy lifting, posing practice, and the diet. The only trouble was I had and have a business to run. I've been blessed to have a full schedule and taking time for *me* has always been an issue. The only time I could see my coach was before work, because my twelve-hour day couldn't be compromised for my hobby sport. Workouts at 4:00 a.m. were the only choice. I did it for three years—the whole wake-up-at-3:00-a.m. thing. This year, I had to make some adjustments to keep the process going because the wake-ups were taking their toll.

Queensland, Australia, actually felt much like Oceanside, California. Well, except the people there had accents. Carl, Dad, and I rallied up and went. I got fifth this time, in the figure open category. I had a fun outside photo shoot afterward, and then we did the whole get-on-the-bus tourist thing again. Being the daddy's girl I am and adoring my husband, I was in heaven being with my two favorite people. Another incredible trip in the books.

The 2019 season arrived, and we returned to South Korea again. My dad was never interested in going to South Korea. Politics got the best of that trip, and suddenly my husband's demeanor toward the entire competing concept came to light. Bodybuilding is a selfish sport. It is. Between the eating, the workouts, and the cost, Carl was getting fed up. I always had to be in bed early for the 4:00 a.m. workouts. We never went out to eat, my emotions ranged from high to low based on how hungry I was, and my sheer obsession over it all was bothering Carl more than he let on. Never once did placing or getting a darn medal fuel my performance. It was more about how I looked and what I had accomplished getting there. The experience was so much different from the year before and left us both really emotional.

The end of that South Korea trip was filled with some really tough heart-to-heart conversations between Carl and me, the types that had ultimatums. We reached a compromise that I would finish the year out, not go to Australia for the world championships again, and then be done. Just be done. I had to, for my husband. My dad had double teamed me on this one. The only person I felt was on my side was my best friend in Colorado, who knew how much I loved being on stage.

When we got home, the fire died out with all this talk of quitting competing, and I told Carl that the promoter in Australia really wanted me to attend. This time it was in Melbourne. I'm an athlete, so the idea of finality—meaning no more coach, no more following a diet, all that structured my day coming to an end—brought tears to my eyes. I was addicted to the sport and felt like I had in the past, figuring out what to do next, as I always had to. It made me sleepless, distraught, and worried.

Forward thinking, and thinking about not competing, didn't settle well. But I felt like I had no choice. Part of me imagined going out to eat, cooking different dinners, having a few rest days, maybe going on vacations, and maybe having a social life. The part of me that craves to do something, the addict part of me, couldn't grasp the upcoming change. Carl could see the sheer grief this was causing me, so he agreed to let me go to Australia with the finality of it being my last show. One more. Okay, well, at least I bought myself some time.

Praise the Lord, Australia went amazingly, and that was just the game changer I needed, not only for myself but for Carl too. After I was awarded second and third places in the entire world, Carl looked at me with total endearment and said, "I'm so proud of you." That meant everything to me in that moment. We left the event center that night and went out to have that culminating cheat meal. While we waited for the food, Carl turned to me and said, "Look, I don't think you have to stop entirely. Maybe one or two shows next year. I mean, you did just get second and third in the world, so you can't really just stop." Hmm, that was all I needed to hear. Thank God.

CHAPTER 42:

Transition and Turmoil

Photo credit Daryl Lane

The summer of 2019 before I headed out to Australia presented challenges, downfalls, and confusion for me, to a degree that I was beginning to lose control. It seemed like the year of disappointments, crashing, and burning. It seemed like my crown was being stripped. Business
was slowing down, and the empty hours of the day left me stir-crazy

and scared. Worry was at an all-time high. I was hardly sleeping, hardly smiling, and hardly living with any type of enjoyment. I couldn't get control of this persistent uneasiness. As someone who despises and tells my clients to never say the word *can't*, I had reached a point of sheer exhaustion and whispering to myself before I went to bed that I hoped I didn't live to see the next day. I kept repeating to myself that I *can't* live like this. I was reaching my end. I was wishing that I wouldn't wake up. My existence was being questioned constantly by the demons in my head that wanted to see me crash, burn, and give up. They were starting to win. They were starting to show themselves to the public, and even I knew it. You see, it's easy to let pride and ego misguide the realities of what is right in front of you. No matter what extent of misery I was experiencing, I refused to go see a doctor or go back on medication. But deep down, I knew I had no choice.

For one, I was a complete bitch to Carl, and secondly, if I didn't rein in it, my clients would soon see, and then that slow downturn in business could lead to my end. I'd tell Carl I wanted to die. I even hit him in frustration that I couldn't figure out how to be okay. I blacked out, yelling at him at the top of my lungs, so angry that he couldn't fix me. When the two most important people in your life (Carl and my dad) tell you they don't even know who you are anymore, the stab stings so bad. The open wound just gets worse and worse.

Finally, I went to the doctor. I had built up worry and anxiety about going, but when the visit took ten minutes, I picked up my prescription on my way home (have to love our pill-popping society), and I felt the calm coming to get through this storm. Maybe I wouldn't be okay that day, but I'll be damned if I didn't look forward to possible relief.

Going back on anti-anxiety medication probably saved my life… again. As someone who thrives on "all natural," it's hard to admit that my wires get loose and I need a little rearranging to get on track. I'm never one for pity parties or playing the victim, so using medication and saying I have a problem seems like a cop-out that makes me a wimp. Truth be told, a true wimp is someone who doesn't go get help. This type of stubborn attitude diminishes quality of life and well-being. People die procrastinating and ignoring their health until it's too late. I was being a hypocrite to my clients by telling them to take care of themselves more, pay attention to their body's needs, and to seek help, when I was turning my back on myself. It was going to be too late for me soon. I had planned a couple of ways to escape this life for good, and soon I would take matters into my own hands.

CHAPTER 43:
One-Sided Treatment

My mental health had been in this place before. It wasn't uncharted territory. My mother had that knack for perfecting us, and I had been seeing a psychiatrist since middle school in an on-and-off manner. During my high school years, I was diagnosed as "depressed," being mistaken for sad because I didn't hang out with friends or go to school dances. The prescription medications at that time may or may not have worked, but they sure did make me tired. I had trouble staying awake and would doze off frequently, but what could teachers say to a straight-A student? I didn't want to say it was my medication, but I didn't want to somehow have this problem reflected in my grades. Falling asleep in class was just another unspoken topic that somehow never stood in my way of doing well academically. Between late night trips to the emergency room and taking medications that numbed me, I was a zombie.

But here's the loop in all of this...until college I had the same psychiatrist as my mom. Our sessions would be scheduled back to back, typically with her going in first. Then I would step in for my turn, walking straight into a line of fire about everything that was wrong with me. Wrong with me? Um, my mother was a raging alcoholic who was taking more than one prescription from you, and unbeknownst to you (or so you said), she was making her own cocktails with these pills and drinks. But I was the sad one, the one who needed to be fixed. Lying becomes second nature to addicts, and just like how she could pull it together when my brother and sister came, my mom could flip that switch for that doctor really quickly. Walk in, talk about everyone else, get the pills she wanted, walk out, my turn, mission accomplished. This form of one-sided treatment went on for four years.

When I left for college, the doctor told me we could do over-the-phone sessions. As if I had any choice. But eventually I did stop answering her calls, and eventually my mom's sporadic attendance to her sessions made this easier for me. Being in an out of rehab and eventually having her driver's license stripped made getting to her office tricky. But don't be fooled—she was on auto-refill for the meds, so that wasn't interrupted. The distance and my mother's inability to even tend to herself allowed me the chance to slip out of treatment and then stop taking antidepressants.

I was surviving college, for the most part. Now in a forced social environment, I struggled on my own. There wasn't the choice to isolate, being that I lived with, ate with, and was constantly surrounded by my teammates. I felt that I was approaching crashing and burning, and all I ever wanted to do during college was go home. Every day was a day that put me one day closer to being home.

I was miserable even before the ACL injury because I could never relax and just be me. All my compulsions and needs had to be hidden or compromised for me to escape judgment. Maybe I was depressed? But I wasn't sad; I was just worried, worried, worried. I could hardly sleep and just wanted to be anywhere but where I was. I needed help but didn't know how to go about it, other than calling my dad. I would also call my sister a lot. Both hinted at me going to the doctor again and returning to medication. My best bet was to look some people up online, give them my insurance card, and try them out. Okay, well, let's see: "Psychiatrists in Denver, Colorado." Guess I'll start with the closest one. Nope, didn't take my insurance. Going by distance and merely pointing and choosing, I finally found one. He was a male, but I was lured by the fact that maybe this was a better fit for me.

He was more than I could have even asked for. Right away he told me that I wasn't sad, but I had anxiety. My constant uneasiness and inability to relax and just be in the moment wasn't about wanting to go cry in the corner. He prescribed medication, and shortly thereafter, I was starting to feel better. I was speaking for myself and telling him my symptoms, not having my mom dictate the treatment. Looking back, thinking of all that I was going through at home, I never once told the psychiatrist we shared the truth about my mom. My mom was her loyal ongoing client. But this time, I was truly getting help. The gray clouds were lifting, and I was starting to see light at the end of the tunnel that I would be graduating early and going back home. Every day was one day closer to getting the hell out of Denver.

Given our medical industry, there are always copays, especially when you see a "specialist." As a college student, I did not have copay money, but I took the option of being billed later. My dad, never being the bill payer, and my mom, now incapable of running the household, left me with billing statements for this doctor starting to add up. He was well aware of the circumstances, being that I opened up everything to him. It was now my turn to say what was going on in my life. When it was time for me to move back home and we had our last few sessions, he told me for the duration of our treatment time together (about one year), He had never been paid. I felt beyond terrible. This man had pulled me off the edge of a cliff for almost a year, and here I was, stiffing him on the bills. I had and still have respect for him.

When I did get home, I did see some of these bills in the mail, and I told my dad that it was really important we pay off this debt to this man. I said, "Look, sign the check and let me mail it to him. The entire amount, Dad." We did. I wrote a note of gratitude and admiration to this doctor because he was someone who finally listened and finally diagnosed me correctly. Maybe there is no such thing as a correct diagnosis when it comes to your mental health, but when the fog lifts, it feels nice to be able to breathe easier for a while. When I moved home, well, it was back to being off meds because now I didn't have to go back to my mom's doctor, and now I didn't have a doctor at all.

Shortly after my mom passed, my dad once again presented the idea that I should go talk to someone. I mean, things like finding your mother dead do call for a dose of therapy, so it seemed like a good decision. I was well aware that what I had seen and been through was well over the top, and even though I didn't know how to feel, I knew that there was a process to overcoming an event like that. I tried a few people. I would start from day one with them, go a couple of times, and just think this wasn't going anywhere. I had "my story," but talk therapy was just talk and no relief. I was tired of reliving the event, and I was tired of the whole question-and-answer formality with no answer making me feel any better than when I had gone in.

Just give me the pills. That has pretty much been my relationship with psychiatry. We can sit in the room and talk about this, circle around and discuss my feelings, but medicine is what I needed and will always need. Unfortunately, the one-and-done method with psychiatrists wasn't leading to any prescription writing because I knew they wanted my money and copays to keep coming back. No meds again for a while, and I would just wait to see how long I could slip by this way again. Time went on and I didn't really face my demons; I just went through the motions of life as I continued to figure out what I wanted to do and grieved—or rather, ignored—the loss of my mother.

Not long after my mom passed, my dad started dating. It was surprising how quickly he entered the dating field, but then again, he hadn't been in the most attentive marriage for the past ten years. Online was the "new thing." To be honest, the first two gals were pretty neat women, but they were short lived. I had to explain to him that even though we were all adults now (my siblings and I), when you bring a woman to family functions, she is lured to believe the relationship is more serious than it is. In fact, when you can't even label it a relationship, I told him that family dinners and holidays are off limits. It was leading women on when all he wanted was a little attention and someone to spend his time with.

He got into a pretty serious five-year relationship and despite my own troubles with that girlfriend (feeling like I needed my dad's attention similar to my mom) she did help me find a psychologist to talk to. I actually really liked talking to this doctor. She had a lot of really great advice. Talking wasn't enough. Hadn't we already concluded this? She gave me the referral, and I did end up seeing a doctor just a few times who filled out the prescriptions for me, and that was the basis of our relationship.

Then I turned twenty-seven and was no longer covered by my dad's insurance. Luckily, I had just gotten married, but the transition from one to the other type of insurance was a long process. I paid for medications out of pocket during the time lapse, until I could no longer cover the two-hundred-plus dollars every refill. The cycle of medication stopped again. Stop and start. Waiting until I needed it and it was almost too late has been my relationship with my mental health. Our mental health system is discouraging and not easy to navigate through, and I attribute many of society's problems to this phenomenon.

I want to share a relevant example of this from one of my recent doctoral research projects. As previously mentioned, I plan to write about my program **PAIPAA**, the Physical Activity Intervention Program for Alcohol Abuse, for my dissertation. I have designed an entire exercise program to be implemented into alcohol treatment programs to use as a coping mechanism and alternative to drinking, which can especially be applied once leaving a facility. But here's the point: I needed to learn about what current programs offer in terms of physical activity. Therefore, I called the six local centers in San Diego to explore this. Using an internet search, each center directs you to an 800 number when you call. This means you are directed to a voice operator with punching numbers and then are transferred once you figure out that you have picked the right option. Then I was placed on hold, waiting for someone to answer until I just finally hung up. So you're telling me that when I have finally made the decision to get help and seek treatment, I call an 800 number and wait and wait until maybe someone will answer? The likelihood of sticking out that call and making something happen is very slim. Of the six, two answered, and of the two, only one called me back after I left a voice mail for the director. I get why people give up, and I get why people feel there is no help.

CHAPTER 44:
Here We Go Again

When I first opened my studio, I was feeling in a good place. I was newly married and newly opening my own business, and here I was, doing what I finally wanted to do. I started out strong, ready to tackle the small business world. Although all my intentions and goals were in the right place and lined up, I made the really mature decision that I better get myself straight and my act together proactively before I hit a wall again. Life had shown it was only a matter of time, every time, before I would find myself ready to check out on everything. Now, being on new insurance, I had to try to find new help.

But again, to make arrangements to see a doctor about my anxiety, gave me anxiety. Number one, do you take my insurance? Number two, you have now placed me on hold or transferred me three times. Number three, I need a referral from my primary care doctor. Number four, you only have these days and times available. Number five, the first available appointment is in three weeks. Then when I get there, there is paperwork, the doctor is never on time, I have to cancel clients to have time to go, and then I have to sit there answering pointless questions to get the prescription. Then I have to stop to the get the prescription. It's just *a lot* to someone who actually has anxiety. No wonder I totally delay the help seeking every damn time.

I took the meds for a couple of years and then recall missing an appointment on accident, merely forgetting about it, and then I just didn't go back. I always do that. I feel like I've got myself totally together, like there is no need for meds. It gets me in trouble eventually. Ask anyone who takes medication for their mental health. There are two perspectives: 1) yes, poor me, I have depression, ADD, PTSD, or whatever, and all this bad stuff happened to me, so now I have to take medication, or 2) I guess I'll take meds since my doctor says so, but I don't really need them (pride, ego, denial). It's hard to find a middle ground because it's not really a private or uncommon condition anymore. People talk more about what is wrong in their lives than what is right (well, except for the falsity of social media).

Think about it. When we ladies talk to our girlfriends, do we tell them how great we are doing? No! We confide in them, ask their advice, spill our guts. We never say, "I'm doing fabulous, no complaints." Every other commercial on TV is for some new medication that convinces us we have those symptoms. The pharmaceutical industry is thriving, and we are masking our issues and popping pills more than ever, me included. Somehow, I think that I actually qualify for these drugs and don't abuse them. It took me a long time to accept the notion that I take one of those meds on those commercials, but hey, I guess living instead of dying is good justification.

I say all this with a little smirk, but medication has literally saved my life *a few times.*

It's funny. Each time I take the meds in that starting-over phase, I share with people how good I'm feeling again. So why do I keep reaching this point of "Oh, I don't need them anymore?" Human nature, I guess. I'm smiling because I'm happy, not pretending to be. That's the reality of owning your own business. You wear that smile every day, no matter how you are actually feeling. There are no off days or sick days; there are "be-there" days—that is, if you want to have a successful business. It ain't easy, but it's a whole lot easier when you smile because you feel good versus the "fake it till you make it" method. You get really good at acting like your personal life is perfect, because ultimately there's a fine line in mixing business with personal matters. I've always felt like admitting to a client that I don't feel well or that I'm really tired is weak. Yes, I'm human, but they see me as the Energizer bunny. One of my clients, who always braids my hair (I love having my hair braided), asked me if I ever have grumpy days since my days are so long. I told her, "On the inside, yes, but you will never know it."

Flash-forward to today and, well, I'm back on meds. I held strong for nearly five years, but I felt the lack of control, the dark haze, and the negative, life-taking thoughts creep their way in and then overtake me again. People always tell me I have so much going on, that I should slow down and get some rest. It's the slowing down part that makes thoughts surface because the silence lets the demons be heard. I fought it and I lost (I always think I will win), so I went to get medication again, jumping through the hoops for that ten-minute chat with the doc to write the prescription. The black cloud started to be lifted soon after, and I was feeling like the person I had worked so hard to become...*again*.

There is a little irony in my medication cycle, seeing as how I get so addicted to objects and routines. Why is it that I can walk away from medication after a certain point? I just let go of it, whereas everything else would require a wrench to pry me to get away. Every time I have gone off meds, I don't get worried about what could happen once the final dose wears off. I just sort of stop, and it's "out of sight, out of mind" with the pills.

CHAPTER 45:

Religion

B ut this time when I hit rock bottom—even deeper than rock bottom, this time—something even more poetic and mystifying happened to me. I asked God for help. You see, I never went to church, and when I did go at a young age, it was because my friends had some sort of Christian teenage hangout function they wanted me to go to. I had never been impressed by religion. My experiences with the titles of Christian, Catholic, Mormon, Jehovah's Witness, and Jewish all seemed hypocritical to me. My attempts at attending Christian and Catholic churches resulted in me feeling like an outcast, feeling judged, and just walking away, thinking it's too late for all this. I had sports every weekend, so we didn't do the Sunday church attendance. In fact, in my family we never even talked or even now talk about religion. At night, my dad would tuck me in, and we would say our prayers. Let's see. It went something like, "Now I lay me down to sleep. I pray the Lord my soul to keep. Thank you, God, for..." The missing factor was that no one ever told me who or what God was. It was just a fun rhyming prayer.

In college, as I started to struggle socially and mentally again, I tried a Catholic church with a teammate a few times. It was a nice experience seeing the beautiful church, but I didn't really relate to the services, having no formal background. During this time period, some of my teammates were also devout Christians who had Bible study together but I had never read the Bible, so I didn't go. Then strike three came after college, when I went to a couple of Catholic services at the mission with my mother-in-law and husband. If you aren't baptized, you are supposed to move out of the way to let those who are worthy go up and take the bread? Thanks for making me feel super-uncomfortable and judged. No thank you.

I just lived by the golden rule: "Treat others how you want to be treated." I felt really solid about the principles my parents had taught me, and remember, I was a really good kid. I felt like everything in life that I had achieved, I had worked for and earned. Maybe there was a higher power, or maybe there wasn't, but karma seemed to serve people the right way who crossed me. I wasn't a "sinner" by any means. When people talked about God to me or said they would pray for me, I just felt weird. Thanks? It just seemed like a catchphrase people used.

But this last time when I hit rock bottom, when it came to finding help, I reached this point of desperation. What could it hurt to try out this God concept? I have a few very strong, influential women in my life who are more than just clients to me. Their concern for my well-being had radiated with the compassionate friendships toward me and their motherly natures. And a couple fed me the whole God thing a few times, saying they were praying for me, saying if I ever wanted to talk about God and their stories, they would be happy to share. It went in one ear and out the other. Maybe that worked for them, but I wasn't open to it. I wasn't ready.

And then, late one Friday afternoon, a client canceled at the last minute. Any disruption to my life at that point and being thrown off schedule was agony to me. I had to fill that hour productively to avoid getting so anxious. I walked my treadmill at the studio and had a conversation with God. I call it a conversation because it went something like this: "Hey, God. Now I don't want to be one of those people who only comes to you when something is wrong, but I don't really know what to do anymore. I'm absolutely miserable, and I don't even want to be here anymore. So I'm going to be open to this idea of a relationship with you, a talking relationship, and just see where it goes." That was the start.

I opened my heart to God and was ready to release my worries, fears, and troubles to him, and in return to receive the outcomes he had planned for me. For once it was realizing that I can't control the outcomes of every situation and the fact that I can't stop thinking about them isn't going to change them. I can't force or make someone do something or act in a certain way. I've learned to ask God for the choice words and the better actions to navigate through challenges. I've also decided that not everything has to be a challenge. Part of this change required me to stop rehearsing life. Constant forward thinking anticipates worry. When I try to foresee what is going to happen, and if the person says this or does that, then I will say or do this or that—no. No more of that. No more of being some delusional director of a play I have no control over. My trust and openness to other people had really been broken. Some of my closest allies had done terrible things to me. Some of my long-term clients stopped coming, and that always leads to never talking again (out of sight, out of mind), and I just felt like the world was full of selfish people. That is why I always worried and predicted the worst outcome.

I'm now understanding that God will bear my burdens for me and not every disappointment is in fact a disappointment. There are lessons and blessings in all that we do. Faith and trust in God and feeling him with me and within me, have absolutely changed my life. I have a confident peace about myself now.

CHAPTER 46:
Family

This revelation opened my heart to the idea of family, which I knew God wanted me to do. I have struggled with the concept of family and just have buried myself in my work and goals. This has to do with my need for structure. Any time I have done things with family (and this is probably true for most people), everything takes forever. To just go see my sister is a three-hour drive. The car part alone is six hours. I've felt like an awful aunt because I don't want to make that trip for a birthday party and turn back around. I don't want to stay the night up there because that throws off my workout and eating, and I have to be at work daily. That entire anticipation is much easier to deal with when you just don't go. My brother lives in New York, so that pretty much takes care of that. When it comes to my husband's family, he is one of seven children, so nothing is short lived. When you have never been around that big family atmosphere, it has made me want to hide because it's just so much for someone who doesn't even hang out with other people. But God has enlightened me that these excuses can be addressed, and that starts with just talking to them more.

In today's world, text messaging isn't that complicated. I do group chats with both my siblings and Carl's family, and not that this is tremendous family time well spent, but when you started at zero, it is something. I will admit that I feel defeated before trying when it comes to both God and family. The whole concept of "too little, too late" comes to mind. You found God at age thirty-three? Too late to start going to church now. With Carl's family I feel like after seven years of being married to their brother, they won't accept that now I want to try to do things with them. And I'm still figuring out what to do with my sister.

Part of me says that she is the one who moved away, and part of me says that it would be kick-ass to be that cool aunt. But her husband has three siblings who live close and serve as amazing aunts and uncles, so I'm way behind the mark. I pray about it, and I think about it a lot, but the cards that God deals with my relationship to family will be played however they are supposed to.

CHAPTER 47

Communication

Photo credit Stephen Smith

My constant communication with God has revealed a life worth living. I actually feel at peace. I actually feel like the silence is okay, and I actually look forward to relaxing. Hard for me to even acknowledge that. I talk to God multiple times throughout the day, discussing my feelings and opening my heart to releasing and then receiving. God wants me to be needy. He wants to hear what I have to say.

I'm not in a place yet, or maybe ever, where I have sought out going to church. The idea of community does appeal to me, but again, as mentioned, I'm in a place right now that I just like to be around family and close friends. It's my trust circle, and in doing so, I don't get hurt by the actions of others. I'm not so worried about what everyone else is doing. I moved into my home that I bought and worked very hard for two years ago. I'm just now domesticating it because I value home as my sanctuary and safe place. Before, I needed to be out and about doing something. Now, I sweep the garage, do dishes, wash all the clothes, organize Tupperware—things that I thought were mindless and ridiculous before. I'm okay, in fact, I'm excited to just be at home. Lighting candles and just sitting in the recliner. I patched up my weaknesses and have sewn wings. I don't even get bored anymore. Thank you, God.

CHAPTER 48:
Today's Perfectionism

Photo credit Kathy Magerkurth

Part of my zest for bodybuilding is to have the perfect body...of course. It's having the muscle and the beauty to match. I work until I like what I see, and when I don't, well, the mind of a perfectionist doesn't settle. What can be done to make the changes, *now*? That comes with pretty much all territories of my life. How to be the best, how to accomplish it all, what to do next. It's a drive and a passion for sure. My choices and priorities are different than many, but is that bad? This doesn't always conform to social norms, but what is normalcy anyway? I haven't had much of it to compare.

Here's an example. Someone has a party. I will go for a short time to be polite because I was invited. But then it is impolite to not stay long, according to others. I have to wake up early because of my goals or work, so staying late isn't ideal for me, but I'm going. It isn't good enough, so then the question becomes why go at all? I feel trapped to stay, and all enjoyment is gone. I hear it from family all the time that it is rude and selfish.

Practically anything that starts at 7:00 p.m. or later is off the table for me. I work seven days a week. Getting home at 10:00 p.m. and then being up by 4:00 a.m. isn't ideal. I have to have the energy to function and have a smile on my face the next morning bright and early. Sure, I like concerts, games, little get-togethers, but during the week, it is super hard, and weekends don't make it much easier.

All of this can be perceived as an excuse, as me being self-centered or just not caring. I never said I was too good to go or above anyone else to participate. I just don't go with the flow. I don't do kinks in the schedule well. Being thrown off one day makes the next day(s) thrown off. I can go do things; they just have to be on my terms, and my terms aren't okay by others' standards. I love concerts and plays and basketball games, but if the start time isn't around 4:00 or maybe 5:00 p.m., then it's too late for me. Then the dilemma becomes that the 4:00 and 5:00 p.m. events require closing up the studio early to get there. These thoughts cause turmoil and sleepless nights, and I have to avoid the RSVP. People do stop inviting and do stop asking. I'm not going to say that I don't take slight offense to this, but it does make it easier for me.

Let's face it. I've never been a bridesmaid (besides my sister), or asked to be a godmother, or had a girls' trip. I've never even had a spa day. I may not have those social practices or occasions in my life, but I have many accomplishments and have achieved a lot. I don't fit the mold, but my mold is pretty admirable. I can't please everyone, and there will always be critics.

The question becomes whether I'm happy or not. I could say yes, and I could say no. I could say that I'm ready to do more, win more, and check more boxes off my to-do list. I could also say that it might be nice to just go to a birthday party and eat cake, meet a girlfriend for lunch, or go have a pedicure and a massage with a girlfriend. Both could be possible, but I haven't bridged that gap yet because it has to be on my terms.

Then there's the whole issue of whether Carl and I are going to have kids. Well, now understanding how hard it is for me to go to a movie past 4:00 p.m., how the hell could I have a kid? Some say it all changes when they are born. Right now, I couldn't imagine putting a workout aside, not being able to shower when I want to, or just sitting at a park watching them play. I would sit there thinking about all I needed to do or could be doing instead of sitting at a park. Responses can be interesting on this. Doesn't Carl want kids? Actually, we are responsible adults and had that discussion prior to marriage. He does not. Won't you be lonely when you are older? I'd like to think I'd have my husband and pugs. Don't you want to see what your child would look like and they would be such a great athlete? Having a kid isn't like having a Barbie doll just to see what he or she would look like and to carry out my athletic dreams.

CHAPTER 49:
My Two Guys

When my addictive patterns are in control and regulated (well, to an extent), which means they are kept more private and to myself, I'm not hurting anyone or being lectured. When the excessive and extreme set in, which is bound to happen, that's when I have had some really harsh, hard talks with the two most influential people in my life: my dad and Carl. When Carl and I were planning to be married, neither of us had religion in our lives at the time, so we did not attend formal premarital classes. We instead met with the very pastor who helped with my mother's service and would perform our ceremony. We went one time, and he blessed our marriage, but I did have a one-on-one conversation with him. He knew me for most of my life through my dad's basketball connections and wanted to make a clear directive to me. Before Carl left the room, he told him the best piece of advice he could give him was to not lock his knees at the altar or he might pass out.

When Carl left the room, I nervously awaited what he had to say. He told me had known me a very long time, and his concern was that I would choose my father over my husband. He explained that Carl was my family now. That meant he came first. Gosh, was that the perception everyone had about me? Of course I more than understood, and believe me, those words are ingrained in my head because the topic does become relevant every now and then. Fortunately, I have been extremely blessed that my husband and dad are close; in fact, they are really good friends.

I love that Carl and my dad are super close, like father and son. However, when I'm not doing well, it does hit hard—pit in the stomach, punch to the gut, slap to the face—when the two people whom you love unconditionally and respect what they have to say the most tell you that you need to make some changes. The worst, absolute worst, was when my dad told me once that he didn't understand why Carl stayed with me. Ouch. Ouch on every level. My life is really consumed by *me*. The studio, school, competitions, working out, eating clean, and then…Carl. And then Carl. Yeah, I know. I can do whatever I want, whenever I want, and Carl goes with the flow. This went on for years, with me not really thinking about whether he actually wanted to do many of things I had to do or caring if I was busy and he was home. Because he is the ultimate homebody now, and because when I'm gone, it allows him to watch his shows, play with the dogs, hang with friends, or play video games, I figured it was a win-win. Not exactly.

Communication is a vital part of any relationship, definitely including marriage. I'm not sure when I decided I could read his mind and assume all was well. Yes, here and there, he said things like "When do we ever do anything I want to do?" But to me it seemed like all he wanted to do was to be at home. I will admit to missing his friends' weddings as his date and not going to work functions of his or other social occasions where having your significant other on hand is protocol. I either had to work or didn't want to stay so late—I mean, really, any excuse. My goals took precedence over time spent somewhere I didn't want to be in the first place. Okay, so yes, it sounds selfish, one sided, not a partnership. This last time, when everything hit the fan in South Korea, and I knew needed to go back on medication; it was not just because I couldn't live with myself, but I knew I was reaching a place where even Carl wouldn't want to be with me.

Ladies and gentlemen, I got a good one when it comes to husbands. That man loves me and would do anything for me. Me reciprocating that has been absent. Most recently, I needed to go back on meds to save myself and my marriage. I was taking a lot of my lack of self-control out on Carl. He was standing in the backyard having his nightcap drink, and I shared with him something that was upsetting me. He didn't respond with the answer I wanted at that very moment, so I slapped the drink out of his hand. I was reacting to his drinking, like how I used to dump my mom's alcohol out. The next night I got upset because I'd had a terrible day. Who knows what he said or did (probably nothing at all), and I sucker punched him. Rage. Almost blackout anger and an out-of-body feeling. I screamed at him that he would regret being mean to me when I killed myself that night. What the hell, Megan? Who was I becoming?

So again, that summer of 2019 was a very low, low point in my life. Luckily, I got back on meds, and best of all I found God. Now, I take pride in being a better wife, and I even do all his laundry and put it away (hey, it's a big step).

CHAPTER 50:
Ideas Become Musts

Photo credit Kathy Magerkurth

S ome people think of things they want to do or see and say that would nice, maybe someday. When I come up with an idea, that means it is going to happen. I'd like to think of this as an admirable trait (ha ha) in the sense that I do what I say I'm going to do. Reliability is one of the foundations of why my business has done well. When I said I should open my own business on a Sunday, I was looking for a space to rent on Monday morning. When I had the idea that I would do a bodybuilding competition, I signed up on December 31 and—bam!—competed in March. When I said I'm going to buy a house, I made an offer that day. When I said I'm going to get my doctorate, I started on the next available date and took the next available entrance exam. Don't give me bait because I will take it. It's the belief that there is nothing I can't do if I set my mind to it.

Okay, so isn't that a great personality trait to have? It's also part of an addictive personality that possesses the quest to do all and see all. It also creates my own perception that other people don't do what they say they are going to do, and I can't rely on anyone because no one lives up to my standards or expectations. It's so far gone that even if I ask my husband to change the laundry, I run home on my lunch break, not believing that he would actually put the clothes in the dryer after telling me he would. This also explains why I have no employees. It's a do-it-all-myself mentality coupled with truly not trusting anyone to do what they say.

I'm a rather get-it-done-myself person, which can make a day much longer and a task more overwhelming. People have to earn my respect and trust, and even then, when I let them in, it's at max capacity at 80 percent with the notion that they will never meet all my requirements. Even people I hire, such as a cleaning person, gardener, pool service, you name it—I expect them to reschedule, not be able to come a certain week, et cetera. Because I never miss, I hold that standard, but this standard can be ruthless.

CHAPTER 51:
Shopping

Photo credit Kathy Magerkurth

I got the shopping bug from my mom. Now, her taste might have been a little more branded than mine, but shopping was something that kept part of our relationship intact. When she was seemingly healthy and sober and I worshipped her in my early years, we shopped like the stores were going to close down. If I had a soccer tournament, in between games we went to the nearest mall. If we were off school (we went on a "round track," which meant two months on, one month off), we readily shopped a few times a week. She didn't mind driving far, either, for the stores she liked. Nordstrom and Macy's were two of her favorites, but the woman could shop anywhere. Even the county fair was fair game to buy every knickknack. The drugstore CVS was even a playing field for her. Cost never seemed to be an issue. What she wanted she got. I wore the latest brands and never was turned down on any item I'd present to her.

When she was sick, we had the "buying my love" phenomenon going on. Take you to an AA meeting? Okay, well let's stop at the mall after, and I can, no problem. Where is your meeting? Oh, okay, that's by Best Buy; we can go there after. It was a negotiation to get what I wanted and for her to not feel so terrible about her current predicament.

Today, my shopping habits are a reflection of the need for more and more. The addict mentality. For a girl who doesn't have a social life, this means workout attire to the max. Every top has a pair of leggings to match and vice versa. Every outfit has a pair of shoes that coordinate. My accessories never falter and include bracelets, necklaces, anklets, and a sports bra that also complements what I'm wearing. I also bring a jacket every day that matches. The key to my shopaholic obsession is going to thrift stores. I love the hunt, love it. Once you get into this habit, anything over five dollars for a shirt is overpriced. Shoes, no more than ten dollars. Most of my tanks are about ninety-five cents or one dollar. Sports bras should be kept under five dollars. Leggings vary, but anything over eight dollars is too much. Jackets are a tough call, but around eight dollars or less is acceptable. Bracelets and jewelry are cheapies for sure. Amazon is my friend too. I call myself an "Amazon whore."

My taste shifted from buying brands with my mom to finding the cheapest best buys. People notice my fashion and compliment it often. When they ask where I got something, every time, they're amazed at my "score" purchase. I don't spend hours in the thrift stores or scrolling online. A person on a schedule doesn't operate that way. I breeze through, in and out, knowing right where to look. Either they have it or they don't. With Amazon, I can debate a little with myself over prices, put items in the shopping cart for later, or buy. I'm an instant gratification shopper, so if it isn't now, it's probably never.

Most workout attire is twenty-five dollars for a tank, and some people spend upward of fifty dollars or more for leggings. I'm like, that's almost twenty-five tanks and at least five sets of leggings for me. It's nice to find a brand name "score," but that doesn't persuade my decision to buy something. This comes in handy big-time when I do photo shoots because if the photographer isn't providing the outfits, I know I'm only going to wear them for a few minutes each. I can make a five-dollar outfit look like a million bucks, and hey, I like going to look for the items requested for the shoot.

CHAPTER 52:
Modeling

Photo credit Lernik Elle Sepanosian

I had a client who was a photographer, and she kept saying I should really do a photo shoot sometime with her. I work so hard for my body, and I should show it off. Well, you see, I can get up on stage in a tiny bikini and pose, accentuating my muscles and being all glammed and tanned. Yet for about the past ten years after college, I didn't even own a bathing suit of my own (like to go in a swimming pool). I even have a swimming pool in my backyard. I've been that trainer who covers it up, doesn't walk around in a sports bra, or really even a pair of shorts. Not that there is anything wrong with wearing a pair of running shorts, but maybe my days of basketball tainted my view of anything that went above the knee. It could be daddy's girl syndrome; I felt like bathing suits were too revealing. I don't know why my mind separated the bodybuilding from wearing a darn bathing suit to the beach, but again, you can convince yourself of anything.

Living two minutes from the beach and seeing it from my upstairs room, I have a true love and appreciation for the ocean. I grew up a mermaid, loving to swim and dive through the waves. I was a junior lifeguard and could hold my own out there. But one summer while I was home from college, when I was at my heaviest weight (but I still went to the beach with my friend), I got stung by a stingray. That did it for me. No more water. I was approaching that point when you have gone out in the water and you are trying to see how deep it is, so you touch your feet down to feel the bottom. *Zap!* Got me. Sliced the bottom of my foot right open. I screamed to my friend, "I think something bit me!" So we swam back to shore, refusing to make contact with the ground. We must have looked like idiots when we got to the sand and were still on our bellies even though the water ended. She ran to get the lifeguard, and I sat there with my bloody foot in a bucket of ice.

My view of the ocean was tainted, and I still enjoyed running and walking by it, but never going in, just admiring it from afar. So you see, there really wasn't any need for a bathing suit anymore. I made a few attempts with water shoes, and people would just say do the stingray shuffle and don't pick up your feet. For anyone who has been stung, the fear persists for reoccurrence. That's the mystery of the ocean. When you can't see the bottom, you really don't ever know what could happen.

Another reason I have avoided the water is the temperature. If I don't even go in my own swimming pool because it is too cold, the ocean certainly isn't going to have any fighting chance. I would need a wetsuit, and that whole process of getting that thing on and off just deters me.

The point to this ocean talk is that I finally did the photo shoot starting out on a boat in the harbor. Having no bathing suits, we did sort of a fitness-themed, rock-hard-body-on-a-boat look. Pretty cool, but by the next one, I did graduate and quickly advanced to posing next to a Ferrari in a bikini. Then with my thriftiness, I went bikini shopping and merely twenty-five dollars later, I had about five suits. Let me tell you, I actually felt attractive and comfortable, and I went in the water. Impressed with myself, and in love with the photos and the response I got from them, I fell in love with the idea of photo shoots. Since that day, I have done plenty more, have sought out photographers, and have been asked to do modeling. My love for the beach has come alive again, and I go at least twice a week.

I've found a new hobby. Modeling has gotten me to love the ocean again, be in the water, embrace being a Southern California girl in my body, go places that have been in my own city but that I've never taken the time to go see, and feel like a woman.

Modeling complements my life of fitness and health. It is really fun to put together ideas, makeup, and locations with photographers, and to come up with outfits that fit the theme. This gives a whole other reason to thrift shop. I grew up shy, attached to my mother's leg, but now I love the camera. I am pretty selective about the photo shoots and make sure the photographers are professional and that I'm in full control of what I'm wearing and doing. The industry can be dangerous, but I'm competent and careful. I've greatly enjoyed this new hobby and purpose.

My mother was extremely beautiful, so this endeavor lets me think, "I got it from my mama."

Photo credit Lernik Elle Sepanosian

Photo credit Kathy Magerkurth

CHAPTER 53:
Finding Peace

Photo credit Kathy Magerkurth

Just being at home, just being, has never been fulfilling to me. Time has to be used purposefully and meaningfully. Naps, no way. Rest and recovery, yes, but actively and efficiently. That means considering doing my homework as rest or writing articles for magazines as recovery. That means making sure that I'm at least sitting with or near my husband or dad or with the pugs while doing so. In my own way, I'm spending time with them while "resting and relaxing." Watching a movie without a side task seems impossible. Sitting still is a miracle. Oh yeah, and everything has to be in its place or complete before even attempting to rest or relax. There is no "do it later." The buzzer went off that the clothes are dry. Pause the movie, interrupt the sentence—I need to go put those away. I really need to make my lunch for tomorrow. We can start the show after I get that done. After. Procrastination has never been associated with my lifestyle.

Now in many ways, this is a positive, right? I do not put things off. With my doctorate courses, the syllabus outlines the entire eight weeks of work. By week four, I'm normally done with it all. I try not to have that overachiever, better-than-everyone-else vibe, so I wait to turn it in, but the work is done. There's no way I could watch a movie knowing that next week something is due, even if it is seven days away. I take advantage of time when time is there. I have no idea how people can wait until the last minute.

Another form of this is how I grocery shop. Now this one gets Carl and my dad. The freezer is filled to the brim with frozen vegetables and the meats I will be eating. There is a true surplus of whatever my coach has dictated as my eating plan for the weeks to come. I have a fear of running out of something and then disrupting my time and having to run to the store at the last minute to get that item. When you always have the foods on hand, meals can be made in advance, allowing a grab-and-go rather than having to stay up later or squeeze in getting the meal packed and made on the same day. If it's Monday and a client canceled at the last minute, even though I just went to the store Friday and have plenty for the week to come, probably two weeks' worth or more, I go to the store Monday because the time is there. That way I don't have to worry that I won't have time later in the week to go. I've cleared the space for other options at the end of the week and checked off one of my to-do list items. It doesn't matter that I probably can prep for the next thirty days with what I have; I have to go to the store once a week. Fortunately, most of what I get is frozen, so I'm not wasting foods. However, let's say my coach adjusts the plan, and I have six bags of mixed vegetables that are now not on the new plan. Well, yes, I'm going to keep those six bags, but now I've got a really full freezer. Addictive nature.

It is silly how just frozen vegetables can get out of hand when you are a perfectionist. I hear it from Carl and dad to stop buying so much, but it's a peace of mind that settles my agenda and allows me to breathe easier. If I'm at work all day, I want to go straight home to my house. I don't want to stop at the store on the way home. I was planning to do my homework or write when I got home, so if I go to the store, that cuts into that time. Every minute has a purpose, and I want to stick to that original plan. Therefore, throw a wrench in the equation like a social activity, and I'm all out of sorts. I had planned to wash all the house rugs Friday after work; then someone asks me to go see a movie. Ah, yes, I could wash the rugs Saturday, but that's not what I had planned on doing. Yes, I'm totally being serious about something like washing floor rugs. And to think you asked me if I'm going to have kids? Ha, funny.

Recently, my peace of mind has reached a new level of clarity and direction that actually involves doing less. Just being has become more comfortable, as the space in my heart and head has opened up to allowing God to provide me with the peace of mind that he will control outcomes. He will provide whatever I need as it should be, at the time it should be, and however the screenplay turns out. I will always aim to change the changeable, but I'm learning to accept the unchangeable. I'm learning that when I release my worries and fears to God, I receive the blessings and actions as they should be. I sleep a lot better now. I don't try to rehearse what comes next. I am in constant communication with God, so that he knows (as if he didn't already know) the direction my mind is wandering so I can get back to peace and clarity. Oh, I steer to the right and left often, but even when I'm running the warm-up with clients, I have a conversation with God to watch over and protect me. He provides me with the choice words and levelheadedness to run my business in a way that I don't feel *so* stressed out.

CHAPTER 54:
Biceps: My Strength

Photo credit Kathy Magerkurth

People see me as strong, inside and out. Let me tell you, I am. I am resilient, stubborn, determined, and ready to take on the world. I'm ready to train celebrities and professional athletes. I'm ready to teach an audience of students at the college level. I'm ready to change lives through movement because movement is medicine. The human body has taught me that you can get up and face the world one step at a time independently, but with a lot more smiles and meaning when you let God take the lead. I love every muscle and vein that I see in the mirror, but I pray daily, several times a day, about inner peace. I still fight taking a rest day or missing a workout. I still count every step and record my Fitbit. I still weigh and take my body fat every morning.

My biceps keep me in line physically, give me a purpose, and let me work out the crazy that makes me sleepless. Physically, I can outlast the best of them. That is what separates me from others. I keep going. The hits, the blows, the aches, the pains, the worries, the fears—my strength is in my ability to show up, no matter what. My dad taught me that sick, tired, ready, or not, you show up. It's the most fitting lesson for owning a business. Now, seven years after starting the studio, I've shown up every day, and I make a living at what I love to do. My passion is my career. Call it an addiction, but fortunately I've found strength in this addiction to change the lives of others for the better with it.

CHAPTER 55:

Butterflies: Her Spirit

Photo credit Stephen Smith

I believe when a person passes, their spirit isn't always ready with the physical body to transition to the next life. With a trauma like my mother's, she wasn't ready to go to heaven, but God called upon her, knowing that he could give her a better life. Carl was the first to see her image after she passed. He saw her in a glowing white light, standing at the foot of our bed. We had moved back into my childhood home after my mom passed because my dad didn't want to live alone and needed help. We left that room we rented together early on in our dating and moved into my parents' home. We were there just a few nights, and Carl saw her. When we woke the next morning, he shared it with me, not in a scared or freaked-out manner. He asked if she had long blond hair, and she definitely did in her babe years. He said she just stood there like she was checking in. He wasn't scared and didn't feel like he needed to wake me up. My sister has shared this same vision.

I have seen her twice but feel her presence all the time. I had just opened my studio, and Carl and I were renting a condo near the beach about five minutes away from my work. Anxiety makes me toss and turn at night, so I move to the couch or guest room all the time in the hope that I'll finally fall asleep. This time I went to the couch. I woke up from a little nap (never a deep sleep) and could feel a force that wouldn't let me sit up. I finally jolted up and saw her. That white glow and long blond hair. Not scary at all. She was healthy and shining in all her beauty.

While walking the beach, during the time period of writing this very book, the sun had set, and the sky was hardly lit. Gazing out into the ocean, I saw her. There she was, with that white light and long blond hair, standing in the ocean, letting the waves surround her. I gasped for air and shed a few happy tears.

Butterflies seem to show up whenever my family is together and all the time when I'm with clients outside. Many can tell you they even land on me. To symbolize this, Carl and I released real butterflies at our wedding. My brother did the honors, and those who knew the importance of this were in awe that one monarch butterfly landed on the flower decor and just stayed. That butterfly stayed to see the moment her daughter was married.

Butterflies are her spirit and are in my presence, checking in on me, flying by when I need a smile, and letting me know there are so many beautiful blessings in my life to be thankful for. Butterflies give me inner peace and enlighten me to believe that I'm okay. I'm okay being Megan. I'm okay to breathe and enjoy being in the moment. I'm okay to let God control the outcome.

My biceps and the butterflies that are surrounding me complete my outer and inner self. I pray for peace several times a day, and the more my faith has grown, the more opportunities my biceps have given me, and the more butterflies I see, the more comfortable I am just sitting and being okay with me and who I have become.

This is my story of addiction and passion. Addiction can come in any form. There's no escape. My mother, Rebecca Fern West Johnson, lived to be fifty-five years of age. Upon finishing this book, her spirit is with me as I have unintentionally ended with Chapter 55.

Like the butterfly, I have the strength and hope that I will emerge from my addictions and be transformed.

I'd love to hear from my readers and help every BODY I can...

To follow me, reach me, or just to check out my day to day life, my social media is included below.

Facebook https://www.facebook.com/megan.johnson.374549
Instagram @megan_everybodysfit
Website https://everybodysfitoceanside.com/
YouTube https://www.youtube.com/channel/UC8yvzvtCObAg4AAlrcV0TfQ